BATH SCHOOL DISASTER

On May 16, 1927, a dynamite blast rocked the Bath Consolidated School and tearing one wing of the building nine children and teachers. Thirty more were injured. An inquest concluded that dynamite had been planted in the basement of the school by Andrew Kehoe, an embittered school board member. Resentful of higher taxes imposed for the school construction and the impending foreclosure on his farm, he took revenge on the citizens by targeting their children. Soon after the explosion, as parents and rescue workers searched through the rubble for the children, Kehoe took his life and the lives of four school officials, including two superintendents, by detonating dynamite in his pickup truck as he sat parked in front of school.

Paranormal Lansing

Schiffer Publishing Ltd

4880 Lower Valley Road, Atglen, Pennsylvania 19310

Nicole Bray
&
Rev. Robert DuShane

Dungeons & Dragons: Originally published by Tactical Studies Rules, Inc. (TSR), later known as TSR Hobbies, Inc. The game is currently published by Wizards of the Coast, a subsidiary of Hasbro.

Ouija is a registered trademark of Parker Brother's Games.

Schiffer Books are available at special discounts for bulk purchases for sales promotions or premiums. Special editions, including personalized covers, corporate imprints, and excerpts can be created in large quantities for special needs. For more information contact the publisher:

Published by Schiffer Publishing Ltd.
4880 Lower Valley Road
Atglen, PA 19310
Phone: (610) 593-1777; Fax: (610) 593-2002
E-mail: Info@schifferbooks.com

For the largest selection of fine reference books on this and related subjects,
please visit our web site at **www.schifferbooks.com**
We are always looking for people to write books on new and related subjects.
If you have an idea for a book
please contact us at the above address.

This book may be purchased from the publisher.
Include $5.00 for shipping.
Please try your bookstore first.
You may write for a free catalog.

In Europe, Schiffer books are distributed by
Bushwood Books
6 Marksbury Ave.
Kew Gardens
Surrey TW9 4JF England
Phone: 44 (0) 20 8392-8585; Fax: 44 (0) 20 8392-9876
E-mail: info@bushwoodbooks.co.uk
Website: www.bushwoodbooks.co.uk
Free postage in the U.K., Europe; air mail at cost.

Copyright © 2009 by Nicole Bray and Rev. Robert DuShane
Library of Congress Control Number: 2008942475

Designed by Mark David Bowyer
Type set in Batik Regular / Zurich BT

ISBN: 978-0-7643-3206-7
Printed in the United States

Contents

Dedications

T o my father who became my favorite ghost-hunting companion. You gave me a lifetime worth of great memories that will always be cherished. It is not the same without you. I miss you, Dad. This one's for you!

—Nicole Bray
Founder of West Michigan Ghost Hunters Society

To my best friend Gary, who never questioned my belief in ghosts, or my desire to hunt for them. I only wish you could have joined me on an investigation in life. You are dearly missed.

—Rev. Robert DuShane
Founder of WPARanormal Inc.

Acknowledgments

S everal people were a great help with this book and they all deserve a "huge pat on the back."
First and foremost would be our official photographer, Bradley Donaldson.
We would also like to thank our researchers and other photographers who helped with this book: Jeff Westover from SwampGasGraphics, Ralph from the Clinton County Genealogy Society, author Mathew Swayne and Colleen Shunk.
Joseph Stewart from the Ghost Research Centre for your investigation submissions.
Dr. John Crisler from the "Man Cave" for his hospitality and contributions.
We would like to extend a huge thanks to Kerry Chartkoff, for the tour most people never get of the Michigan State Capitol building.
Julie Rathsack and Terri Snow for editing work.
Last, but definitely not least, we would also like to extend a special thank you for all those that emailed us with research information or allowed us to include your haunted houses in this book.

Introduction

Everyone seems to think that ghost hunting is glamorous and exciting. Yes, everyone has seen TAPS on *Ghost Hunters* by now, and many are in awe of the fame and excitement. From time to time, it can be exciting when you get a spectacular piece of evidence captured on audio or video. So paranormal investigating can have its adrenaline-rushed moments, but scurrying around a dirty, moldy basement is never glamorous. The majority of the time, it is time consuming and just downright boring. With twenty combined years of paranormal experience between us, we have certainly seen it all!

Hollywood has been known to depict, from time to time, ghost hunters as scientists with nuclear packs strapped to our bodies, satanic cult members, or shamans that fall into trances every investigation. This is the farthest from the truth. We are everyday normal people. We work full-time jobs, pay bills, and take care of our families. The only difference between real paranormal investigators and the general population is that we have a second job that takes us to the edge of recognized science.

What you are about to read is a compilation of haunted locations, ghost legends, and other strange experiences from Lansing, Michigan, and its surrounding towns. Some of these locations and legends remain a mystery to this day. Others have been debunked, and some just simply got away.

We as the authors would like to remind you to always obtain permission before you perform a paranormal investigation, as some of the locations mentioned in this book are private property. Trust me, it's not worth being arrested for an hour or two of ghost hunting!

We hope you enjoy this book and Happy Haunting!

1
Lansing's
Shady Beginnings

It might seem odd to think that parts of Lansing, Michigan, started out as an elaborate fraud, but in fact that is where the Michigan State capital's strange origins lie. One would never guess that the sixth largest city in Michigan was nothing but worthless swampland back in 1835.

Years after the area was first surveyed in 1925, two brothers from Lansing, New York, plotted the area just south of current downtown Lansing and gave it the name of "Biddle City." The entire area was laying in a flood plain and was underwater the majority of the year. The two brothers returned to New York State in early 1836, and began to sell plots of land in this make-believe city. Not only did they fail to tell the patrons that the city was underwater, but also embellished tales of the city fostering a church, a public square, and town area of sixty-five blocks.

Sixteen unfortunate men from the state of New York believed the brothers' smooth sales pitch and bought plots of land in this fantasized utopian city. Later that year, with dreams and ideals for a new life, the families reached Biddle City only to discover that they had fallen victim to an elaborate fraud. Either too disappointed or too destitute to return to New York, the approximately twenty people stayed in the area. Each family claimed additional land and managed to turn Biddle city into a functional township. In honor of their hometown in New York, they renamed the area Lansing Township.

The War of 1812 had a huge impact on the state of Michigan. The decision to move the state capital to a more centralized location came because of the fact that British-controlled Canada captured the city of Detroit, which was at that time the capital of Michigan.

Several days' sessions commenced. Many cities in Michigan wanted the honor of being the state's new capital, and lobbied hard for it. There were many cities in the running; the list included: Jackson, Marshall, and Calumet. Tired of political wrangling, the House of Representatives, out of pure frustration, decided the new state capital would be Lansing Township. When the decision was publicized, hearty laughter ensued. Most people found it absurd that such a small insignificant village could become the capital of Michigan. Two months later, the laughter subsided when Governor William L. Greenly signed into law the act that made Lansing Township the new Michigan State capital.

In 1848, the small individual settlements near the Grand River were dormant no more and new developments began to emerge. By 1859, the settlement grew, the population soared to over 3,000 citizens, and the once-tiny Biddle City now covered approximately seven square miles. The city of Lansing, the capital of Michigan, was born.

Here are some of the more interesting portions of Lansing's timeline. Some of the events mentioned actually tie into some of the supernatural locations and events that you will find further in this book.

1825 — Lansing Township surveyed.

1836 — A group of New York speculators plot and market a non-existent city known as "Biddle City." The New Yorkers that bought into the idea arrive in Lansing to only to discover that the plots they had bought are located in a marsh, and are underwater. Some of the pioneers stay, but develop a village in what is now Old Town Lansing, a mile north of the non-existent "Biddle City."

1847 — The state capital moved from Detroit to Lansing Township.

1855 — Michigan State University founded as the Agricultural College of the State of Michigan.

1859 — The city of Lansing officially incorporated with about 3,000 citizens inside of 7.5 square miles.

1879 — New State Capitol dedicated. The structure cost $1,510,130.

1897 — Ransom E. Olds drives his first car down a Lansing street. He would later found Oldsmobile, which would become a General Motors division in 1908, and Diamond REO.

1904 — The "most extensive flood in 135 years of local history" causes the Grand River to overflow its banks in March 24-27, leading to major damage and one death. Bridges at Logan Street, Kalamazoo Street, Cedar Street, and Mt. Hope Road washed away. The Kalamazoo Street Bridge became lodged against the Michigan Avenue Bridge; it was later salvaged and re-erected.

1940 — Lansing's population stagnates, only rising by 356 over the decade to 78,753.

1954 — Frandor Mall opens; this was the area's first mall; and only the second in the state.

1965 — The city reaches 33.3 square miles (86.2 km^2) in size.

1989 — The Library of Michigan and Historical Center near the Capitol Complex dedicated.

1992 — The Michigan State Capitol completes an extensive renovation to restore it to its original grandeur.

2004 — Last Oldsmobile rolls off the assembly line at Lansing Car Assembly on April 29th.

With a current population of over 119,000 residents, mixed with its colorful beginnings, it seems inevitable that Lansing, Michigan, would be home to many restless spirits and paranormal phenomena. If you want to find the ghosts of Lansing, we are going to tell you were to look.

2
Ghosts of
Capitol's Past

I f the theory that death, especially several of them, is what makes a place haunted, then the State of Michigan's Capitol building should be literally filled with ghostly activity and specters.

Michigan Capitol Building, 2008. *Courtesy of Colleen Shunk.*

A long-standing rumor states that Indians cursed the majestic Capitol building in Lansing and the visitors to this cursed land are doomed to die. This seems to be just urban legend, since research into the property where the Capitol building is located uncovered no hint of an Indian village or burial ground. In fact, the historian for the Capitol building confirmed our findings that this land was never a documented permanent village for the Natives. However, with the four deaths connected to the building, it is not surprising the Capitol is haunted.

The first death occurred during the original construction of the Capitol building. In the early days of modern construction, there were many serious accidents. Most of these injuries were the results of falls, scaffolding failures, or the occasional stone dropped as it was hoisted into place. Diggary Geakes, for example, became injured when a large stone fell and broke his arm in 1877. On another occasion, the head of the construction firm was injured, although not seriously. Even the architect was not immune to injury during the construction phase of this famous building.

On July 28, 1875, one of these serious accidents resulted in a death. Thirty-year-old construction worker, Thomas Zamosky, became the Capitol building's first victim. Working on the third-story exterior, the scaffolding collapsed and Thomas fell to the second story, breaking his back. Thomas did not die on the scene, but in fact suffered for almost two years until he died of his injuries on May 25, 1877. Thomas never saw the Capitol's completion in 1881.

Shortly after the completion, tragedy struck again, but this time it involved a child. Members of government often hired teenage boys as messengers or "pages." When the messengers were not busy running errands and performing other duties, their boredom soon turned toward mischievous games. One day, while the House was in session, one young messenger decided to take a little nap on a balcony situated over the House Speaker's chair. While in deep slumber, the young man rolled right off the balcony and landed on top of the speaker, and other members of Congress. No one was seriously hurt, but the young boy was humiliated and sent home to his parents for proper punishment.

The boys' foolish games continued until February 10, 1881, when thirteen-year-old Bert Clippenger, a messenger for the House of Representatives, became the second fatality in the Capitol building's short history. According to February 12th edition of the *Lansing Republican*, Bert was playing with a number

The site of Bert Clippenger's tragic fall in 1881.
Courtesy of Robert DuShane.

of other boys on the fourth floor, when he fell four floors to his death.

What exactly he was doing is still unknown, but it was common for them to slide down the banisters or, on dare, to jump the gap from one banister to the next, the local historian believes that he was likely doing the later when he slipped and fell.

The building supervisor, A.L. Bours made this statement about the messenger's tragic death:

"The sad fate of young Clippenger, who while engaged in natural boyish play, was suddenly hurried into eternity, ought to provide a warning to both to parents and children. But will it be heeded?"

Bours pleaded with parents to keep their children out of the Capitol building.

Today, the messengers consist of young men and women who attend college full time. The story of Bert is rarely ever mentioned, especially during the school tours.

Deaths at the Capitol building took a quiet reprieve for fifty-five years, until the year 1936, when David Altman was fatally injured while he was working on the east elevator. Apparently, after touching a live wire, he fell three stories down the elevator shaft. David died in the hospital the next day.

The elevator where David Altman died in 1936. *Courtesy of Colleen Shunk.*

Fifty-six years passed before the curse of death made another visit to the Capitol. In 1989, work to restore the Capitol building back to its original beauty enjoyed in the late 1800s began. Artisans worked long hours during this restoration process.

On March 31, 1992, one craftsman, fifty-two year-old James Parady from Midland, Michigan, was working on the restoration of the exterior copper roof of this magnificent building, when for some unknown reason he decided to detach his safety harness. This unfortunate lapse in judgment resulted in his untimely demise. Apparently trip-ping on a ledge or eas-ily losing his balance, James fell off the top of the Capitol building and onto the concrete ninety feet below. No one saw the accident happen, but his death affected many of his co-workers and friends at the state's Capitol.

The site where James Parady fell to his death in 1992. *Courtesy of Colleen Shunk.*

In November of 1992, during the rededication of the Capitol, a plaque was unveiled, commemorating those who had given their lives in the original construction, maintenance, and restoration of the building. The plaque features the deaths of Mr. Zamosky, Mr. Altman, and Mr. Parady. The story of young Clippenger's death was not known at that time of the rededication ceremony.

With these four tragic deaths, taking place in one building, it is inevitable that stories would surface about ghostly apparitions of the doomed men and the male adolescent.

Is this building haunted? While doing interviews of visitors and employees of the Capitol building, not one person claimed to have experienced anything remotely close to paranormal activity. If you do a Web search for paranormal teams that have claimed to have "investigated" the Capitol building, you will find that they in fact just participated in the normal daytime tour of the building, and only came away with the typical photos of orbs.

Orbs have been thought by some to be "spirit balls" or the beginning energy form of a spirit. There is, perhaps, a five percent possibily that these "orbs" might be more than dust and moisture particles captured on film (especially with digital photography). But unfortunately, outside of these photographic anomalies, nothing has been documented to support other tales of ghosts of Michigan's Capitol building.

Nevertheless, that will never stop the ghost stories from circulating. People have speculated for years that while you are surrounded by the portraits of former governors (in one of these portraits, the governor appears as a specter himself); you are also surrounded by the dead. Visit the beautiful Capitol building and decide for yourself. Haunted by ghosts or just haunted by its heartbreaking past.

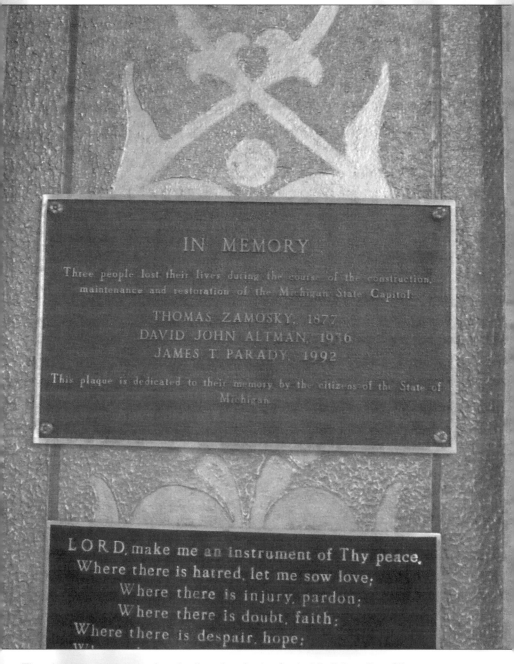

The plaque commemorating the lives lost in the Capitol Building. Bert Clippenger was not named on this plaque. *Courtesy of Robert DuShane.*

3
Michigan
State University

O ne often wonders if higher education also means higher levels of paranormal activity. No one can dispute that just about every American university campus boasts residential ghosts and strange tales of the supernatural. Many adults just dismiss this notion and blame it on too much alcohol and drug use, or the over imaginative minds of young adults.

Michigan State University (MSU) is like many other university campuses across the United States. Founded in 1855 as an agricultural college, it underwent several name changes until 1964 when it was awarded the final name of Michigan State University. MSU's first classes began on May 14, 1857 with sixty-three students, five faculty members and three buildings, all of which are now nonexistent.

How things have certainly have changed. Current enrollment consists of approximately 44,000 students with over 20,000 currently living on campus. The University's alumni include governors, senators, and ambassadors—not to mention such legendary people as John Ramsey, father of murdered Jon Benet Ramsey; James P. Hoffa, son of Jimmy Hoffa; and Bubba Smith from the *Police Academy* movies. Actress Angelina Jolie and pop singer Christina Aguilera both completed online and correspondence courses through MSU. Another notable figure was one of its first graduates, Lieutenant Gilbert Dickey, who served with the 24th Michigan Regiment, commonly called the

"Iron Brigade" during the Civil War. Lieutenant Dickey was mortally wounded during the first day of the Battle of Gettysburg on McPherson Ridge, not far from where his commanding officer, General Reynolds, lost his life. This brave Lieutenant lays in rest at the National Cemetery in Gettysburg, Pennsylvania.

Michigan State University is also well known for its unique history and strange artifacts. Nestled in the MSU Museum archives in the Central Services Building, is one of the world's largest bovine hairballs; it was extracted from a dairy cow in 1985. One can only imagine what other unknown artifacts are hidden in these archives, yet to be discovered by the public.

In 2003, University spokesperson Terry Denbow was quoted in the *State News* as saying, "I think legends, myths, and reality all combine to give a campus texture and flavor. This campus is full of traditions because every generation adds or detracts from a story."

Michigan State University is definitely surrounded by myths, legends, and numerous hauntings. No one knows how many unseen denizens are walking among the student body in the campus halls, or reside in the dormitories of this immense university campus. Stories and eyewitness accounts of ghosts have spooked students for decades. A former MSU senior wrote a human-interest story for the *State News* in October 2001. In it he stated, "Maybe it's just me, but for some mysterious reason, there seems to be a death on the campus of MSU each year. I sometimes think that MSU was built on an ancient burial ground."

Interviews with students and faculty offered a couple quotes that sum everything up concisely about deaths at MSU.

"When I was entering into MSU as a freshman," the student explained, "I was told that every year, a student drowns in the river and someone gets hit by the train. They are mostly alcohol related fatalities, but it all held true. A student died at MSU every year I was there."

During an interview with a maintenance worker, he exclaimed, "I wouldn't be surprised if MSU has tons of spirits walking around. Every hall on this campus has had at least one death take place inside it."

Simon Bronner, professor of folklore at Penn State University has been quoted as saying, "college campus ghosts, in contrast with those said to haunt graveyards, are thought of more as residents than as bullies. There aren't many campus ghost stories in which the ghost is threatening residents." Perhaps Mr. Bronner is correct about that, but that does not stop the students from becoming frightened by their experiences with the supernatural and the knowledge that they have to share their campus with the unknown.

Mayo Hall

One of the most notorious hauntings on the Michigan State University campus is centered in Mayo Hall. Built in 1931, the hall was named in honor of Mary Mayo. Born on a farm near Battle Creek, she was the wife of a Michigan Senator, and an activist that promoted education for women at MSU. Mrs. Mayo was also a teacher of women's studies at the Michigan Agricultural College in 1897.

Mayo Hall, 2007. *Courtesy of Brad Donaldson.*

Additionally, she advocated for the first women's dormitory. Because Mary was a determined lady when it came to the topic of women's rights and privileges, the men of Abbott Hall was booted out of their building and it was converted into classrooms and housing for women's programs. Later, the college also built a new building for the program, Morrill Hall, in 1899.

Although Mary died twenty-eight years before the Hall opened, and neither Mary nor her children ever resided at the Hall, it does not stop the legends and reports of Mary haunting the darkened floors of Mayo Hall.

Through the years, there have been many stories circulating of how Mary died and came to haunt this particular location. Some of the most popular descriptions of Mary's demise were that both she and another female student committed suicide in the basement. Mary was murdered on the fourth floor, and yet another tale places her murder scene in the basement. However, no one can forget the ever-popular story of Mary hanging herself from the rafters in the attic of Mayo Hall.

In truth, Mary did not commit suicide nor did she die by the hands of a maniac murderer inside the halls or basement of Mayo Hall. Mary died in April of 1903, from an "incurable disease" and now rests with her husband, former 7th District State Senator Perry Mayo, in Austin Cemetery in Calhoun County. None of Mary's children has ever lived in the women's dormitory hall.

Even though in life Mary never was aware that a Hall was dedicated to her memory, generations of MSU students claim that she roams the halls after her death.

An unlucky pizza delivery worker had the unfortunate experience of walking through the basement access into the Hall when the campus lost power in the spring of 2006. He stated, "The second the lights shut off, the entire hall became freezing cold, and for no reason, this cold breeze just picked up, and it felt like someone was there. I felt someone touch me. It could have been just the breeze, but it was a grazing that hit my back. I ran the heck out of there."

One unlucky student had a disturbing experience in the laundry room. A nursing senior was in the middle of doing her weekly laundry when a noise arose from the basement corridor. When she investigated this eerie clatter, she found nothing. She commented that it felt like someone was watching and following her, and that "it didn't feel right." This female student is not the only one. Many residents have labeled the basement as "creepy" and often refuse to use the basement that links both sides of the Hall.

Mayo Hall's fourth floor holds its own urban legends. This area of Mayo Hall is reported to be locked, contains boarded-up windows, and can only be accessed by the hall's middle staircase, however a researcher for this book was able to obtain permission to enter this forbidden floor. From the third floor, it is possible to see one of the fourth floor windows, but you cannot see inside. What secrets or legends are held in this student-restricted area with no warmth of sunlight?

Some students have given a section of the fourth floor a name — the "Red Room." The nickname name was derived by the continuous reports and tales of satanic rituals being performed, along with other demonic activities on the fourth floor throughout the years.

A second story with the fourth floor that continues to add some fuel to the fire is the report from a resident aide that a female student committed suicide by hanging, another version of the story states that she was murdered by a fellow student. Either way, the RA thinks that this is the reason for the floor being closed off by administration. Several students, living on the third floor, have complained about tapping and knocking noises coming from the ceiling. Some of the residents have gone further and claimed that the knocking noises from the above floor will follow them out of their rooms.

Anyone who has enough courage can try to prove or disprove an additional fourth floor urban legend of Mayo Hall. Brave souls can place a penny in front of the attic door. If you push the penny under the door, the "entity" in the attic will push the penny back under the door toward you.

The lounge is said to hold an entity that has been spotted standing near the piano or tinkering with the keys, creating a macabre melody. A male student walked out the door of the west lounge. While departing, he noticed nothing out of place. Outside, he realized that he had forgotten his cell phone and re-entered the west lounge to retrieve it. Upon passing the lounge, he immediately noticed that all the chairs, not nailed to the ground, were overturned. Not one sound was made from the lounge while this disruption occurred. The unmanned piano in Mayo Hall is well known for its eerie cords coming from an unseen player.

The forbidden fourth floor of Mayo Hall, 2008. *Courtesy of Colleen Shunk.*

Both the MSU news entities *The State News* and *The Big Green* have continuously written articles and included testimonials from students that have watched doors, and particularly windows, opening by themselves. There is a short amateur video circulating the internet that was created and posted by user "SpartySecrets" that is named "The Haunting of Mayo Hall." In this short film, one student discusses a window incident that happening in front of her and one other student.

A night receptionist was quoted in an article as saying: "A lot of people who have lived in Mayo Hall have reported hearings things like knocking coming from the walls or the closets and not being able to figure out where the noises were coming from."

Not even the bathrooms are exempt from supernatural happenings. A female resident was brushing her teeth in one of the bathrooms when all of the faucets suddenly turned on. With mild hesitation, she turned all of the faucets off. When she turned to face the mirror to finish her daily hygiene ritual, she heard an eerie creaking noise and watched in horror as all the faucets turned back on again. The student ran from the bathroom and was forever haunted by her experience.

In 2007, MSU senior Corey Becker, a former Mayo Hall resident, and some friends created the "Mayo Hall Ghost Hunting Squad." This small society devoted a portion of their time investigating some of the claims and signs of the supernatural in the darkened Hall. They were given access into all areas of Mayo Hall including the notorious fourth floor. Even though many theorize that the MHGHS was only looking for a scare, they came away from their investigation with only disappointment. As Mr. Becker stated about their forays in Mayo Hall, "We never saw anything we thought was supernatural." In addition, for any reader who is interested in the fourth floor, according to the article and the resident receptionist, it looks like a huge attic with insulation, catwalks, fans, and some writing on the walls.

Even if it seemed boring and disappointing to the MHGHS members, I can tell you as a paranormal investigator myself, their sketch describes about three quarters of all attics that I have seen in reputed haunted locations and in many occasions. Once you add infrared video and digital audio recorders, some of those disappointing attics aren't so disappointing anymore!

Mayo Hall may hold the most famous haunting on the Michigan State University campus, but other accounts of paranormal activity, as well as the tragic endings that may have caused them, have been reported from numerous campus locations.

The basement corridor in Mayo Hall, 2008. *Courtesy of Colleen Shunk.*

Fairchild Auditorium

Fairchild Theater, built in 1937, was named after English Professor George T. Fairchild and has its own resident ghosts.

One of the ghosts in question is not of Mr. Fairchild, but that of an unknown little boy, a.k.a. "The Phantom of Fairchild Auditorium." Theater students and building workers tell of a small boy that is often seen roaming the halls, while other students have claimed to have caught a glimpse of his face staring out of a third-floor window. Ghostly footsteps and other unusual noises have been heard from the stage area.

Theater junior Mark Falconer was told of the Auditorium's notorious spirits when he was a freshman. "I heard from upperclassman that there are hallways in the second and third floors where people have heard whispering voices and steps coming up from behind them."

In October 2003, Brad Mikulka and his paranormal team investigated Fairchild Theater. Mikulka, who claims to have the ability to "sense" spirit activity, described a presence in the projection booth of a short man, very old, with blue bib overalls. A stage manager, who was present for the investigation, said that the description reminded her of Craig Chapin, a projectionist who died two years prior. Could the spirit of Mr. Chapin still haunt the projection room of Fairchild Theater? Many believe so.

Brad Mikulka's team documented the majority of his findings in the old projector booth. Other workers at the theater talk about the unknown noises that emanate from the stage area. A theatre associate professor describes one such incident that sticks in his memory.

"I was in the theater over Christmas break working by myself. Suddenly, there was a shuffling noise from the stage area and then you can hear vocal noises. This was nothing that could have been structural. This was enough to spook me out."

Fairchild Auditorium, 2007. *Courtesy of Brad Donaldson.*

Holmes Hall

Home to the Lyman Briggs College, the largest hall on Michigan State University campus, holds 1,250 residents. The Hall is split up into two separate buildings, East Holmes Hall and West Holmes Hall. Amidst the over 1,200 residents, there are also several entities believed to roam the halls of both buildings.

West Holmes Hall's resident ghost resides on the sixth floor and seems to have an obsession with the elevator. Numerous students throughout the years have witnessed a male apparition entering into the elevator. The doors would close and then immediately reopen. Anyone brave enough to look into the elevator would find it empty. The elevator never appears to leave the sixth floor with the man inside; he just simply disappears, only to resume his nightly visits to the elevators for years to come. Numerous other students have reported strange behavior from the elevators as well.

Perhaps this entity is also responsible for the student's experiences with a plethora of strange electrical disturbances such as appliances, stereo equipment, and lights turning on and off on their own.

East Holmes Hall's reputed haunting takes place on the sixth floor and involves the area surrounding the elevator. The nightly encounters with the Hall's two apparitions reportedly take place after 3 am. Described by residents as two shadowy black figures, they are spotted walking into both elevators, where an icy breeze is felt blowing out from the elevators before the doors close. It is unknown if these two denizens ever leave the area of the elevator shafts of East Holmes Hall, but I am sure several students don't ever want to find out.

A small mention in a *The Big Green* news article stated that several Holmes Hall residents say they have tried to catch the ghost, but have

not yet been successful. With the amount of experiences coming from Holmes Hall, maybe someday their luck will change.

East and West Holmes Hall, 2007. *Courtesy of Brad Donaldson.*

Hubbard Hall

Hubbard Hall, whose residents likes to boast about being the tallest hall on campus, is also located in the haunted East Circle of the MSU campus. The center of this Hall is Sparty's Retail Store where students can purchase snacks, drinks, and clothes. What the students will also tell you is that Hubbard Hall holds paranormal activity.

Upon floor twelve of Hubbard Hall, there is a myriad of reported ghost activity. Once again, another Hall in the East Circle has a problem with an entity that loves the elevators. This entity will enter the elevator on the twelfth floor, ride it down to the ninth floor, where anyone unfortunate enough to be standing by the elevator entrance, will experience a cold wind coming off the elevator as soon as the doors open up.

Perhaps this is the same entity that is said to cause poltergeist activity throughout the Hall. Decades of student residents have whispered about doors and windows opening, then slamming shut, lights going on and off, not to mention the disturbing sounds of someone running up and down the halls. Laughter from an unknown source is commonplace among the students roaming the halls at night. Several students have testified on MSU message boards about hearing the sounds of someone running up and down the halls on the twelfth floor. Upon investigating, no one could ever be found to explain all the noise. One resident, who was unlucky enough to have a room that was located by the elevator, often complained of the constant noise of someone unseen walking past his door and getting onto the elevator.

One student admitted to having strange and discomforting experiences and dreams since taking up residence on the twelfth floor of Hubbard Hall. For several nights, this student experienced dreams like those that he never had before. In this dream world, there was a gentleman by the name of "Charlie" who would come into his room while the student was sleeping. "Charlie" would climb on top of the now terrified student and attempt to suffocate him. Each time the student would wake up short of breath.

Naptime for this student was not too much different. Often, upon waking from short afternoon naps, he would find trash from his trash bin neatly lined up on the floor in his room.

This same student also commented that keeping doors opened in Hubbard Hall was a fruitless effort for students because the doors would always close on their own, and without any explanation as to why. The same could be said for the lighting in middle section of the hallway. Unexplainably, the lights would turn on and off on their own accord.

Hubbard Halls, 2007. *Courtesy of Brad Donaldson.*

Williams Hall

Is the name "Williams" cursed? One has to wonder when this is the second building named Williams Hall on the MSU campus. Williams Hall was the second dormitory built on the MSU campus. Named for president Joseph R. Williams, the hall was built in 1869. On January 1, 1919, the fifty-year-old structure was consumed by fire. Due to the holiday break, no one was in the Hall when it burned and no one was injured. In 1937, a new Williams Hall was built.

Williams Hall is rumored as another "hotbed" of paranormal activity on the campus of MSU. Reports from students stretch from witnessing ghostly figures walking amongst the hallways, dancing in the Hall's former cafeteria, to voices and knocking noises have been encountered by students from unoccupied rooms. Many residents have complained of televisions and computers turning themselves on and off during all hours of the day or night.

An email from Cynthia, a former MSU student, described how she would be studying late into the night when suddenly her television would turn on. A little disturbed, she would turn it off and attempt to return to her work.

"Within thirty seconds, the television would turn itself back on again. One time, the television turned on, flipped through the channels, and turn off again. The whole room would have a very heavy feeling while this was occurring. It would stop as quickly as it started, but it would terrify me nonetheless."

Old Horticulture Garden

In the middle of East Circle Drive, there is a park-like area that is apparently teeming with paranormal activity. One would never guess that this peaceful looking area would seem to be the stomping grounds of a male entity. Students for years have reported a dark figure walking about or remaining stationary in the garden area. According to the *Shadowlands Haunted Places Index for Michigan*, some students have also reported the sounds of someone screaming.

During our visit to the MSU campus in July, we talked with one employee who had her own ghostly encounter. During the spring of 2007, she arrived at Agriculture Hall one rainy morning, and while heading up the stairs, she noticed a man standing in the parking lot, near the south side of the Garden. The man was wearing pants, shirt, and a hat that was reminiscent of the 1920s or 30s. She claimed that the man just stood there looking at her, despite all the rain that was coming down. Uncomfortable by this unwelcomed visitor, she quickly entered the Hall. When she turned around at the door, he was gone.

An email that we received from another former student named Anissa claimed to have possibly witnessed the same male apparition, but this time, he was standing near the center of the Garden. The male entity, dressed in "old clothing," stood stationary but was staring at the female student until it disappeared a few seconds later. In August 2007, we received an email from a person who claimed to have psychic ability and encountered strange "vibrations" from the area. This person could only describe this feeling as: "something is not right here; something dark."

Old Horticulture Garden, 2007. *Courtesy of Brad Donaldson.*

The Mysterious Tunnels

Michigan State University has a 10.5-mile tunnel system that connects various halls, other buildings on campus, and continues down to the Red Cedar River. Some of the tunnels are ninety years old and run underneath both north and south campuses. They are mostly used by maintenance workers, but these tunnels hold their own stories and legends.

In a *State News* article April of 2003, MSU maintenance employee Bill McCreary has worked the tunnels since 1968. He was quoted in the news article saying, "There were kids that went down in the tunnels and played that—what-do-you-call-it?—game with tunnels. I don't remember what happened, but it seems that one of the kids got killed or something."

University Engineer Bob Nestle, in the same *State News* article, briefly discussed the problem of students playing in the tunnels. "It's been about 15 years since people have broken into the tunnels in search of a good place to play Dungeons & Dragons. That game got really popular for a while and the tunnels were a real attraction for people who wanted to play that game."

According to local stories of the 1980s, a young male student, a very lonely child prodigy, was obsessively involved with the fantasy role-playing game. His choice of location for his fantasy life was the tunnels under Case Hall. Deep into depression, the young student slowly substituted his fantasy world for reality. As his unstable mental health worsened, he committed suicide in the tunnels by way of sleeping pills. Many say that he is the entity that now haunts the tunnels.

Case Hall Manager Tim Knight confirmed that a student of MSU did continuously play Dungeons & Dragons in the steam tunnels outside of Case Hall. We will discuss some of the events that took place during these games in our later chapter on Dungeons and Dragons.

Most students know that the student in the legend did not die in the tunnels in a doomed fantasy game, however, numerous students still openly admit that they feel that the tunnels are haunted. Many students have described unexplained banging noises and voices coming from the tunnels at all hours of the night.

The Red Cedar River

Can spirits communicate with the living to help locate their bodies? Research on this matter is obviously still up in the air, but amateur psychic, "Christie," believes so. She submitted her experience to the Ghost Hunters of Southern Michigan Web site and is as follows:

"A couple of years ago, a student at MSU disappeared on New Year's Eve. It was a big deal since there were fliers everywhere talking about him and asking people to call if they knew where he was. His picture touched me. He had a kind face and bright lively eyes. I wanted to help very badly, so since I was beginning to develop psychic abilities, I thought perhaps that me and my friends could find him. We started wandering the MSU campus looking for signs of him anywhere, trying to use our ESP to locate the missing man. Finally, we arrived at the banks of the river, and as my friends wandered off, I stopped to lean against a willow tree. As I touched my brow to its trunk, I hear the words, 'he's in the river.' I felt very sad and I told my friends that there was no point in looking anymore. He was dead and in the river. They didn't believe me because the river had already been searched. Three days later, I saw on the news how they found his body in the river after the ice had thawed a bit. The pictures on the TV looked like the area close to where I had been when I heard the voice."

The young man she was referring to was not a student of MSU, but rather someone attending a party at a nearby apartment. Twenty-one-year old Kettering University student Ryan Getz became separated from his friends on New Year's Eve, 1997. Searches for the young man turned up nothing until a Saturday afternoon in April 1998. Ryan's body was discovered floating amidst the thawing ice patches in the Red Cedar River. The official cause of death was drowning due to intoxication.

In October 2001, Eric Blair was a Bay City resident who also disappeared from an East Lansing party. His remains were found in the Red Cedar River, by Waters Edge Drive, four days after he was reported missing.

Not too far from Waters Edge Drive, and very close to the Red Cedar River, a couple of former MSU students made a brief mention of an MSU student who committed suicide by hanging in the 1980s in the Sanford Natural Area, behind Holmes Hall.

Are the spirits of the dead doomed to walk along the edge of the very river where they perished? Some people who are sensitive to the vibrations of the spiritual world claim that is exactly what is happening. Therefore, if you want to see a ghost, maybe you should partake in a walk along the Red Cedar River at night.

Red Cedar River, near Waters Edge Road, 2008. *Courtesy of Colleen Shunk.*

Wonders Hall

In September of 1999, students of South Wonders Hall began to notice a foul odor. Many residents attempted to investigate the source of this horrible odor, but with little success. Finally, based on numerous complaints, a maintenance employee was able to follow the smell to the basement area. At 2 pm on September 22, this unfortunate employee discovered a badly decomposed body in an unlocked storage room. The body was later identified as Neftali Valdez Greene Jr., an MSU student. Mr. Greene was found in a cramped unused refrigeration unit. Despite that, the situation surrounding the death was suspicious to say the least, the authorities declared this macabre incident as an accidental death by suffocation.

Since 1999, stories have circulated that student residents can hear an unexplained banging noise coming from the tunnel under Wonders Hall. Many people have speculated that it is the ghost of Mr. Greene trying to make his presence known so his body can be located. Perhaps it is the residual sound of this poor student, banging on the door, trying to escape from the refrigeration unit. No one will ever know for sure. A female student posted on a message board about seeing a ghostly figure of a young man wandering around Wonders Hall just a few short weeks after the body was discovered.

The fall of 1999 also presented another tragedy for residents of Wonders Hall. A very well-loved MSU student went home for the weekend and committed suicide. This was a shock to many students, as this gentleman had never shown any signs of depression. One student summed up everyone's feelings as a "life-altering moment for most of us." This death may have also been life altering for those not ready to face the world of the paranormal.

Three days after the funeral of this beloved student, another male resident, walking the hallways at 1 am, spotted a young man that bore a striking resemblance to his late friend. He even describes his gentleman as still having "the jean and flannel shirt that the dead kid always wore." Confused, he whistled at this guy and then shouted out his friend's name. The figure turned to stare at him, and then proceeded to walk around the bend. Stunned, the man could only run towards this strange young man and find out his identity. When he arrived at the bend, there was no one in the hallway. Knowing that he never heard a door open or close, he knew for certain that he had just witnessed the ghost of his late friend.

Another former student in Wonders Hall made his presence know after he passed away. This young man went home for the holidays, and when he returned back to school for the new semester, he was quite sick and it was obvious that something was terribly wrong. He was diagnosed with Leukemia and sadly, this horrible disease claimed its victim soon after. On the evening following his funeral, this charismatic young man made his presence known to his fellow resident friends.

The first person to feel his presence was his former roommate. This roommate describes, while sitting alone and depressed in his room, he watched as the bathroom door suddenly opened up by itself and a feeling of peace permeated the room. The surviving roommate knew that it was his late friend, letting him know that he was okay. The next day, other friends of the deceased student, congregated to report tales of weird phone calls and other strange occurrences throughout Wonders Hall that night. Nevertheless, all residents came away from their experiences with the same feelings of peace and certainty that their friend came back to say goodbye.

Linton Hall

Linton Hall is a very impressive looking building that was erected in 1881, and named after Registrar Robert S. Linton. Linton Hall, the oldest academic hall on the MSU campus, was originally built as a library and museum. The first inhabitant was the president of the

State Agricultural College of Michigan; the first floor was a library and a reading room, and the second floor was originally an eclectic museum, lecture room, and a laboratory for the department of Zoology and Entomology. It was not until 1969 that the Hall was named after Registrar Linton.

Visitors to Linton Hall have talked about unexplained strange noises for years. Knocking noises from unseen locations and the sounds of disembodied voices in The Victorian Era section are commonplace amongst the artifacts.

One former custodian had much to say about her time spent at Linton Hall. Even though she admits to never seeing a ghost at Linton Hall, she is sure they were keeping her company while working in the building late at night.

Linton Hall, 2008. *Courtesy of Colleen Shunk.*

"There are lots of ghosts," Karon Wood said. "You know that feeling you get when someone's watching you?" Karon has often testified that she feels the spirits watching her and that, on more than one occasion, has heard the sounds of them rustling past her. "I know they're here, but I know they're friendly."

Whether the ghosts of Linton Hall are attached to the numerous artifacts that grace the rooms, or maybe a previous student or professor that continues to roam the building, visitors and workers agree that Linton Hall has its share of ghostly denizens.

Emmons Hall
(Brody Complex)

I had a mighty good laugh when I found a reference to a towel-stealing ghost at Emmons Hall. Shaking my head with a smile, I dismissed it as college pranks and left it at that. However, within a six-month period, I came across more references to the same phenomena happening in the same hall, spanning over two generations of students. Now I was a little intrigued. As a paranormal investigator, I am familiar with items disappearing, and sometimes reappearing in an odd location, as symptoms of a haunting. I have though, never came across a ghost that was obsessed with mostly one object — towels!

The first reference I came across was on an MSU message board. The former student was describing his experience with the ghost thief. It was early in the morning when this unlucky student decided to take his routine shower. Upon rinsing off the last remnants of soap and shampoo, he went to reach for his towel, when his hand came across the empty brass hook. Wiping his eyes for a second look, he peered his head once again out the shower curtain in time to witness a shadowy figure moving towards the shower room door and then through the closed door. Looking back down at the hook, his stripped towel and room key were now missing. This student testifies that his towel and room key were never seen again.

Since reading that posting, I came across nine other references, either on message boards or in direct emails. The oldest experienced mentioned took place in 1963, just eight years after the complex was built. This man told of several towels being stolen while he was in the shower. During one such incident, he decided to open the door to see if he could spot the culprit. He was stunned to see a "blackish-foggy figure" silently moving down the hallway and then vanishing.

Young people, who were unfortunate enough to have a towel-stealing episode with this mischievous phantom, have never seen their towels again.

Preliminary research on this freshman dormitory could only dig up a few sexual assaults of female students, but no actual deaths taking place inside Emmons Hall could be found. It looks like the identity of this towel thief will never be discovered; it will always remain a mysterious and humorous addition to the Emmons Hall tradition.

MSU's Eerie Honorable Mentions

This section is dedicated to the remaining reputed haunted areas of Michigan State University campus that spawned nothing more than a brief mention of possible paranormal activity, regardless if real or not. This section also contains college urban legends, and tales of dark spooky areas that prey upon our imaginations!

Physical Plant

The diminutive rumor of this particular building is that a man had once killed seventeen puppies. Interviews with MSU employees have turned up no knowledge of a mass puppy murder. But even with this lack of validity, people posting on online message boards still claim to hear the sounds of puppies "screaming out" as if in pain and a male apparition is reported to be walking around the basement of this building.

Physical Plant, 2007. *Courtesy of Brad Donaldson*

Railroad Tracks

In the beginning, I was not going to add this as a portion of MSU's past, but then several emails from current students and alumni changed my mind.

The early part 1997 was an emotional year for MSU students and faculty. Six students on campus committed suicide or died of accidental deaths in a short three-month period. A few of these deaths were students who were "accidentally hit by the train." Okay, you probably just had my first thought, too. How are you accidentally hit by a train? Did you not see or hear it coming? I am suspecting that the accidents were a horrible result of student dares.

Dreadfully, some of these deaths were no accidents. Over half of these episodes were students who had made the permanent decision to take their own lives. According to a former student, one of these disheartened individuals was a cousin of famous Major League Baseball player, Derek Jeter. This young student hung himself from a tree by the railroad tracks. His swaying body was spotted by a train conductor the next day.

When some emails started pouring in about a male apparition being spotted walking around the tracks at Trowbridge Road, I expected to uncover a story about a death on the railroad tracks at some fraction of MSU's history. I was not prepared to hear about six deaths.

It is sad to imagine that these lost souls may not have moved on to a better place, but are possibly trapped at the scenes of where they ended their own existences on this Earth.

Fee Hall

There is one MSU rumor that is undeniably true; dead bodies do reside in this once-hectic student dormitory.

Fee Hall, built on land that was previously a cattle pasture, was originally constructed as a residence hall in the mid 1960s. The structure that once had 1,200 students now holds cadavers for the Nursing, Veterinary, Osteopathic, and Human Medicines departments. Converted to its new use in 1981, the once bustling cafeteria is now home for the Gross Anatomy Lab, where cadavers are stored for medical research.

Another disturbing thought is that during the transition from a full-out residence hall to a medical research hall, some students had to live in Fee Hall while the renovations were still taking place. I am sure that the remaining residents were very eager to relocate when it became a daily event to witness dead bodies being brought into the building, and some students complained of embalming fluid leaking from the second floor labs into the first floor rooms. Charming.

Mason-Abbot Hall

A former resident of Mason-Abbot exclaimed on an MSU message board that the hall was filled with ghostly visitors.

"There is a sinister, evil presence in the Abbot lobby. Very dark and disturbing. That one (entity) used to scare the hell out of the night receptionists. There is also a female presence in the Stevens T. Mason room in the basement."

Many students claimed to have heard footsteps from an unseen source walking near the area of the night receptionist's desk and the door to the front desk area of Abbot Hall would open and close at night, without any explanation.

A second former resident of Mason-Abbot Hall seemed to confirm the theory that the Mason room in the basement may hold an unseen denizen.

"The Stevens T. Mason room in the basement was always creepy! People claimed to have seen the ghostly image of a woman cleaning down there late at night. That place was definitely scary!"

Mason-Abbot Hall, 2007. *Courtesy of Brad Donaldson.*

Morrill Hall

Here is the briefest of all honorable mentions for MSU. This was a very simple and small message that stated:

"Morrill Hall is haunted. Weird stuff has been going on there."

Nothing more, nothing less. No further contact with the author could be made and no former residents of this Hall came forward with their ghostly tales.

Conclusion

Therefore, in closing this chapter, MSU has staked the claim for being the most haunted location in East Lansing, Michigan. If you ask the many students of this fine institution, they will tell you that they have no doubt in their minds that this claim is truly accurate.

4

Bath
School Disaster

May 18, 1927, started out the same as any other day in May. The sun was shining down on rich farmlands, grassy valleys, and the small town of Bath, Michigan. Mothers finished up the breakfast chores as their children began the walk to the local Bath Consolidated School. The graduating seniors enjoyed the rare treat of sleeping in; it was commencement week and they were not scheduled to attend school until later in the day.

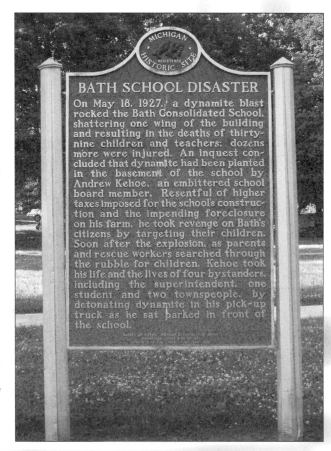

BATH SCHOOL DISASTER

On May 18, 1927, a dynamite blast rocked the Bath Consolidated School, shattering one wing of the building and resulting in the deaths of thirty-nine children and teachers; dozens more were injured. An inquest concluded that dynamite had been planted in the basement of the school by Andrew Kehoe, an embittered school board member. Resentful of higher taxes imposed for the school's construction and the impending foreclosure on his farm, he took revenge on Bath's citizens by targeting their children. Soon after the explosion, as parents and rescue workers searched through the rubble for children, Kehoe took his life and the lives of four bystanders, including the superintendent, one student and two townspeople, by detonating dynamite in his pick-up truck as he sat parked in front of the school.

Historical marker at Bath Memorial Park, 2007. *Courtesy of Brad Donaldson.*

No one imagined that at 9:45 that morning the worst child mass-murder in the history of the United States would begin. By the end of the day, forty-five people (including thirty-six children) would be killed.

On February 1, 1872, in Tecumseh, Michigan, Andrew Kehoe was born into a large family. In all, he had twelve brothers and sisters. His mother died unexpectedly when he was still young. His father remarried a woman that Andrew did not get along with most of the time. To avoid her, he spent a lot of time out in the barn tinkering with machines. This became his favorite hobby.

His psychotic, revengeful behavior became apparent early in his childhood. When he was fourteen, his stepmother, who had just returned from a day in town, set about to start dinner. When she attempted to light the family's stove, it exploded, soaking her with oil, and igniting her into flames. Andrew witnessed what had happened. His initial reaction, however, was to watch her literally burn alive for several minutes before he decided to help. In his own time, he dumped a bucket of water on her. She later died from the injuries. While it was apparent that someone had tampered with the oven, Andrew was never charged.

While attending Michigan State College (now Michigan State University), he met Ellen "Nellie" Price. They married in 1912, and settled on a 185-acre farm outside the village of Bath. Andrew was never a successful farmer. He spent too much time trying to rig his tractor to take the easy way out, and not enough time on the hard work and dedication it took to have flourishing crops. His lack of effort eventually caught up with him. He had no crops to sell, but still had a mortgage to pay.

Neighbors regarded Kehoe as an intelligent, yet short-tempered, man who frequently grew impatient and angry with them when he did not get his way. He was known to be cruel to his farm animals, at one point beating his horse to death. He dressed well and was over-obsessed with neatness, often changing his clothes midday if he saw even the tiniest blemish on them.

Nellie, on the other hand, was noted as a laid-back, pleasant woman. She obviously had a good deal of patience, having to deal with her quirky husband. She had many friends and her neighbors all thought she was a lovely individual.

Despite his own financial problems, Andrew had a reputation for thriftiness. In 1924, he was elected treasurer of Bath Consolidated School. Never one to hold his tongue, he repeatedly accused the superintendent, Emory Huyck, of financial mismanagements. When he could not get his way, he would make a motion to end the meeting.

In the spring of 1925, the township clerk passed away. Andrew was appointed as her replacement until the next spring election. The following spring, he ran for the position, but was defeated largely because of his reputation as a troublemaker on the school board.

Around this time, his wife Nellie was suffering with tuberculosis and had frequent hospital stays. The hospital bills added to the family debt and Andrew's rising resentment. Unreasonably, he solely blamed the taxes that stemmed from improvements made to the school for his financial troubles. His farm fell into foreclosure because he refused to pay the mortgage, insurance, or property taxes. This financial hardship was likely the last straw that pushed him into a decision to punish all of Bath for his personal failures.

It is believed that Kehoe hashed a plan to blow up the school in 1925. Beginning in June, he began to make frequent purchases of pyrotol, an incendiary, and boxes of dynamite bought on different dates from several locations. Even though many neighbors knew of Kehoe's cruel ways and fast temper, no one questioned these purchases from Lansing or his intentions. He found the perfect opportunity to put his plan into motion when he was put in charge of routine maintenance inside of the school building in the winter of 1926. As Kehoe performed periodic repairs at the school, he rigged up the explosives.

The Day Before

Nellie was discharged from the hospital on May 16, two days before the school bombing. Sometime between coming home from the hospital and the bombing of the school, Kehoe went on his own personal rampage on his farm, house, and sadly, his wife. He killed Nellie by a blunt force trauma to her head (determined later at her autopsy). He then placed her body in a wheelbarrow and put her behind the chicken coop. Then, Kehoe girdled up all the fruit and shade trees on the property, and secured every farm animal to posts to insure no escape. Homemade firebombs were placed throughout the farm. He loaded the back of his car with metal debris such as old tools, nails, rusted pieces of machinery, screws, bolts, and anything else that could be used as shrapnel. After the backseat was filled, Kehoe placed a large deposit of dynamite behind the front seats.

The Day of the Bombing

At approximately 8:45 am, Kehoe detonated the bombs on his farm. Neighbors heard the blasts and noticed the smoke in the sky. As they rushed towards the scene to lend a hand, they heard another explosion come from the direction of the school building. Rescuers originally on the way to Kehoe's farm, now turned around and rushed to the school.

When they arrived, the helpers found the north wing of the school collapsed, the walls crumbled, and the roof fallen to the ground. Parts of children's legs, arms, and heads covered with dust and blood, could be viewed sticking out from under the debris. Together, the neighbors attempted to lift the roof to free some of the children, but were unsuccessful. The scene was chaotic. Hysterical mothers arrived at the ruins begging for information on their children, while simultaneously searching through the dead bodies lying on the grass. More than 100 villagers gathered to tear away the debris in hopes of finding any survivors that they could.

Teachers who had survived the bombing described their classroom scene as chil-

Bath Consolidated School, day of the bombing, 1927.
Courtesy of Bath School Museum.

dren, desks, and books flying through the air. Some children were tossed high in the air while others were catapulted out of the building.

Bodies of the dead were lined up in the nearby yards and covered with sheets and blankets. Sobbing mothers were seen holding the bodies of their children, praying to God to bring them back. One mother sat on a grassy hill with one dead daughter on each side of her, as she held her boy, who later died at the hospital. Those children were Vivian (10), Iola (13), and Percy (12) Hart. In a matter of four hours, the unfortunate mother lost all three of her children. Other mothers were crying with relief at having found their children alive. As if this tragedy was not bad enough, Kehoe was not done with his insane act of revenge.

Third Explosion

About thirty minutes after the explosion at the school, Kehoe arrived on the scene and parked his car at the curb. He spotted one of his many "enemies," the school superintendent, across the street. He summoned Emory Huyck over to his car. Eyewitnesses say that once

Mr. Huyck reached the vehicle, Kehoe pulled out a shotgun and fired into the back seat igniting the dynamite. The result was an explosion that killed several others, including the superintendent, postmaster, the postmaster's father-in-law, and Kehoe himself. One traumatized second-grade student who had survived the bombing was running for home. Shrapnel from Kehoe's vehicle killed him.

It is believed that Andrew Kehoe detonated the school bomb from his car by a coil. Upon further investigation, the State Police found 500 pounds of unlit dynamite in the south wing of the school. The first blast most likely short-circuited the line to the second, preventing the remainder of the school's explosion. If all the bombs had exploded, there was no doubt that all the children and teachers inside would have been decimated.

The following day, investigators arrived at Kehoe's farm and found the charred body of Nellie Kehoe still in the wheelbarrow. She was burnt beyond recognition and could only be identified by her false teeth. Tied to one of the remaining fences, the investigators came upon Kehoe's chilling last words on a piece of paper. It read, "Criminals are made, not born."

Paranormal Activity Today

Sites of traumatic events are typically high on the scale for paranormal activity—granted, there are exceptions to every rule. The site where the Bath Consolidated School once stood is a Mecca for professional paranormal investigators and amateur ghost hunters. Hardly a soul exists that is not emotionally moved by the trauma and terror that once took place at this now peaceful park. Some are overcome with feelings of sadness or sudden depression upon entering the property, while others have described having a suffocating feeling or headaches. Many visitors have had to leave the area because the feelings were so intense.

The undamaged bell tower from the original school stands in the middle of the park. This is the only piece of the original school that remains (other than fragments of foundation buried in the grass). Paranormal investigators believe that this is the most active section of the park. One paranormal team placed motion detectors in a perimeter around the bell tower and then walked away in an attempt to gain evidence from other areas. After some time, they heard the chilling sounds of the motion detectors' alarms sounding off. Upon reaching the bell tower, they discovered that the motion detectors were going off, one right after the other. They had perfect domino-effect timing, like someone were walking in front of them one right after the other. Was it an entity circling the bell tower? It sure seemed so! The unexplained activity continued for approximately three minutes and then ceased completely, leaving the investigators astounded.

Bath Memorial Park. The bell tower (shown on left) is all that remains of the original school, 2007. *Courtesy of Brad Donaldson.*

Camera malfunctions are a neverending dilemma for paranormal investigators at this site. Flashes quit working or lights on camcorders suddenly turn off. It is believed by investigators that spirits need energy to manifest. To get that energy, they drain it from the atmosphere and if close enough, from batteries as well. Batteries have a habit of not lasting long at the former Bath school site.

Several paranormal investigators and psychically sensitive visitors say that they can feel the spirits of the children and claim to have been physically touched by them. One entity, believed to be a young boy, has been sensed near a small group of pine trees and bushes. Parahaunt, a Michigan paranormal research team, states that video surveillance has recorded a "ball of light" moving from the pine trees to the bushes. The same team, using an EMF detector, has claimed that they have tracked the young entity.

A few people have reported to see small, dark figures roaming about the park. Capturing EVPs (electronic voice phenomena) is never out of the question from this location as many teams have stated success with this form of evidence.

Unexplained temperature variances, also known as "cold spots," are another commonplace occurrence at this location. Beyond Paranormal Investigations described a baseline temperature reading of fivty-one degrees Fahrenheit, but when an investigator moved his arm about two feet to the left, he amazingly watched the temperature drop down to a chilly thirty-nine degrees.

Are spirits of children that were murdered by a madman still haunting the site of their former school? Paranormal investigators and lay believers alike seem to agree that eighty years later, energy from the children sadly still remains at the location of the disaster.

Memorial plaque at former Bath Consolidated School site, 2007. *Courtesy of Brad Donaldson.*

5

Lansing's Haunted Urban Legends

Blood Cemetery

I f you have ever researched ghosts in the Lansing area, you have undoubtedly read the following story. Not only was this testimony sent to us, it was also submitted to various websites, and was featured in a local newspaper: the *DeWitt-Bath Review* on October 26, 2003. His story depicts a legend that spans across decades of time, but never loses its ghostly charm.

"My name is Drew, and in late August in 1966, two friends of mine, Dan and Tom, asked me to go with them to a party on the beach at Lake Michigan. I was about fifteen years old at that time. Ghost stories were being told around the campfire by almost everyone there, most of which I had already heard.

"As the night went on a young girl, about seventeen years old started telling a story about a family of Doctors with the last name of Blood. It was out on Round Lake Road near Dewitt, Michigan, about 100 miles from the beach party, but only 20 miles from my home in Lansing. The Bloods had a lot of land where the whole family lived. The most interesting part was that they had a private graveyard on the property and that the whole area was haunted. She said that she saw gravestones that dated back to1800.

Blood Cemetery, 2007. *Courtesy of Brad Donaldson.*

"On their prom night, she and some of her friends decided to go out to the Cemetery. They looked around at the headstones for a while. As it started to get dark, the fog hung thick, and a full moon was rising, so they started trying to scare each other. Then the young girl's prom date decided to go into Dr. Blood's house because he thought no one lived there any longer. They waited about an hour or so, and when he did not return, they were scared and headed for the Dewitt Police Department. When they went in to tell the police, the officer on duty said, 'Don't you kids know any better; old Dr. Blood lives out there and he doesn't like anyone trespassing on his property.' He also went onto say that he thought 'Dr. Blood was harmless and he's in his 80s' so, he didn't think there would be any problem. They all returned to the property, but to everyone's shock when they got back, the whole house were ablaze. The fire department was called, but in vane, because the house burnt to the ground. The next day there was a search party, but the only thing that was found in the rubble were the remains of the young man who had gone into the house the night before. The paper reported that his hands and feet had been bound. Dr. Blood's remains were never found.

"One of the searchers that afternoon found a freshly dug grave; when they unearthed it, a pine coffin was found. Upon opening it, they found the body of Mrs. Blood. She was dressed in a red gown, with her arms, legs, and head cut off. There had been no coroner's report of a body being buried there, or any police report of any murder.

"The girl at the campfire that night said that the ghost of Dr Blood, to this day, roams the cemetery at night, with a shotgun in one hand, and an ax in the other.

"That night was the last time I ever heard or saw the young girl who first told me about Blood Cemetery, but it wouldn't be my last experience with the Blood family."

Drew's Personal Story

After I returned from Lake Michigan, I told some of my friends the story I had heard, some told me there own stories, about how they had been scared out at the cemetery. Mark said he had seen a ghost of an old man wandering the graveyard as if he was lost. Another friend said that he saw an apparition of an elderly man carrying a body and it appeared to be headless and arm less.

Another two years would go by, before I got the nerve to visit this so-called haunted cemetery. You see, I never quite believed these "ghost stories," until I saw the most blood-chilling things myself.

The first time I went there was with Dan and JC. It was a steamy hot July night. The moon was big and full and it lit up the night sky as if it were daylight; the fog was drifting over the cemetery as it rolled in from the lake. The feeling in the air was electrifying.

At the entrance to the cemetery were two old rusted iron gates, and hanging above was a sign saying Blood Cemetery. By the light of the moon, you could see the old gravestones. Some had been toppled over, and some were broken. The weeds were about knee high. There was a smell of jasmine in the air.

After looking around for a few minutes, I decided to scare the two of them. I had taken one of my mother's old white nightgowns and I hung it from a fence post when I was sure they weren't looking. There was a slight breeze in the air that night and I thought it would look like it was floating in the breeze. Just as I was about to put my plan into action, I heard JC scream. Dan and I went running over, he told us that he had seen a woman's figure in a long red gown. He said that she appeared to be headless and armless, and was coming right toward him, when she disappeared into thin air. I thought that he had seen the gown I had hung on the post. I took Dan and JC over to see where I had hung the old nightgown, and surely what JC saw was my little joke, but when we got there the gown was gone.

Feeling a little spooked from what JC had thought he'd seen, we started our way out of the cemetery to leave. On our way out, I said to Dan, who was quite a bit taller than me, pull the sign down, and we'll take it home with us.

Our night at Blood Cemetery was pretty uneventful, except for the woman in the red gown. We went back to Dan's farmhouse, where he lived with his Mom, Dad, two brothers, and three sisters. It was late when we got there, so the three of us went to bed, after putting the sign on top of Dan's dresser. The next morning when we got up, we had breakfast and got cleaned up; Dan told his father about the sign we took the night before. With instant anger, his father demanded to see the sign. But this task proved not to be so easy, because when we went to the bedroom to get it, IT WAS GONE. Dan questioned his brothers and sisters, and they all swore they hadn't seen it, let alone taken it.

After a couple of days of looking, we were sure that Dan's brothers and sister's had nothing to do with the missing sign. We drove back out to Round Lake. When we got to the cemetery, there it was; hanging above the old rusty gates was the sign we had taken two nights before, looking like it had never been disturbed.

Several more years had gone by, when I ran into some friends at a restaurant, on Halloween night. They talked me into going out there again. (After all, it was Halloween!) When we got there, the weeds were about chest high and the fences were falling down. One of the guys in the group called us over; he was shining his flashlight on a headstone. We couldn't believe what we were seeing. There lying over the grave was a large piece of glass about six feet long, and about two feet deep, encased in it were a dozen long stem roses imbedded in the center.

Just about that time we heard a shotgun blast. We ran back to our vehicles, and the right side of Dan's car had been shot, and the windows had been shattered. Needless to say we got the hell out of there. With people seeing ghosts, hearing things, and the car being shot up, I swore I would never go back out there again. But I've learned you should never say never.

When I was about twenty-six or twenty-seven years old, I was riding with some motorcycle enthusiasts. It was a beautiful June day; the skies were blue and clear. It was hot, but who cares when you're on your bike. My girl friend, Chris, rode with me on the back of my bike. She had heard so many stories about the Blood family, she decided to bring a camera with her. We looked around at the rundown graveyard, and Chris was taking pictures. After a few hours, we decided to leave, and all of us started down Round Lake Road. We were about 150 yards from the cemetery and Chris and I hit a snapping turtle. The bike went out of control and we crashed into a tree. I suffered only minor injuries, but Chris had broken her back, and was paralyzed from the waist down. She was able to walk again after a couple of years, with the aid of crutches. The curse of Blood Cemetery had struck again.

I've since heard lots of stories since our terrible accident. In 1989, two high school girls were out to have some fun on Halloween night. The news reported that their car went out of control about a quarter of a mile from the cemetery. Their car plunged into Round Lake and they both drowned. The county has now put up hurricane fence around the cemetery, with razor wire strung along the top.

I've learned that at least four or five Blood sons from each generation have become doctors for the last 150 years, and that a couple of years ago, Lansing named one of their Halloween haunted house's after Blood Cemetery.

If you're ever out on Round Lake Rd, and you see a full moon rising, don't visit Blood Cemetery.

As a young investigator starting out with the Kalamazoo Ghost Club, I was drawn to this location, in no small part because of the story of a crazy doctor haunting the site. Like most beginning ghost hunters, I ignored the posted hours and entered the site after hours. I had to know if the Dr. Blood was real.

I took hundreds of photos and hours of audio, I had to prove the ghost was there. We captured several high quality EVP and figured those EVP along with the hundreds of orb pictures we captured proved the legend to be true.

Mission Accomplished.

Fast forward a few years, after outgrowing the commando-style cemetery ghost hunts and actually learning how to collect and analyze evidence, I realized the orbs are almost guaranteed to have been caused by moisture in the air, and the EVP, although real, proved nothing more than it was probable "someone" was in the cemetery.

Close-up of the Blood family gravestone; Blood Cemetery, 2007. *Courtesy of Brad Donaldson.*

My mission to prove the legend true became one instead to re-search all ghost legends before accepting them as facts.

An e-mail to the local historical society inquiring about the mysterious Dr. Blood confirmed my feeling that this story was more legend than history. An email response from a Clinton County Historical Society volunteer reads as follows:

> "I checked the occupations of all Bloods from 1850 to 1950 in the U.S. census reports and none of them were listed as physicians or doctors."

This led me to wonder how many other local ghost legends might be disapproved with some research. As a onetime gifted student and medieval re-enactor, the next legend to research seemed obvious.

Dallas Egbert, the boy who many say died in the steam tunnels while playing a live action role playing version of Dungeons & Dragons.

Dungeons & Dragons Legend

Dungeons & Dragons (D&D) is a surreal role-playing game where players become a mischievous elf, a strong warrior, or even a powerful wizard, traveling to mysterious lands and fighting monsters. Growing in popularity in the late 1970s, this unique game spawned two MSU urban legends.

The first legend states that various students were playing a live-action version of the game in the tunnels when something went horribly wrong and a participant died as a result. The second tells of a young male prodigy who became so deeply involved with the game that he started having trouble distinguishing reality from fantasy. When his character died in the fantasy world, the loss was so real to him, his real world fell apart, and he committed suicide. Either one of these legends could have led parents to want this game banned.

Few people remember that both of these Dungeons & Dragons urban legends are based on a real person who once resided in East Lansing, Michigan. Even the prodigy who enrolled at Michigan State University in the late 1970s would never have calculated that his life would inspire a movie and a huge role-playing public debate.

James Dallas Egbert III (known as Dallas Egbert) was born in Dayton, Ohio. An expert on computers, he was even hired at the age of twelve to repair a computer system for the United States Air Force.

Dallas enrolled at Michigan State University at the age of sixteen, where he had trouble making friends and adjusting to campus life. A big fan of science fiction and fantasy, he joined a group of students who played a "live version" of Dungeons Dragons in the steam tunnels under MSU buildings.

Dallas suffered from severe depression, and while depression is normally a chemical imbalance, many blamed it on his lack of friends, others on the pressure placed on him by an over-bearing mother. The psychologist who treated Dallas when he attended Michigan State University stated, "Dallas suffered parental pressure, criticism, academic pressure, and the failure of all persons to realize that, although Dallas Egbert was a genius, he was socially retarded, and in some respects, could be considered mentally retarded."

Those who want to place the blame on the parents often site a particularly troubling interaction that took place in August 1979. Having received his grades, Dallas called his mother and told her how happy he was that he earned a 3.5 in Computer Science. However, his mother did not share this happiness instead, she scolded him for not receiving a perfect 4.0.

With the constant suffocation by his parents, Dallas turned to D&D and drugs as a means of escape. Dallas was a gifted chemist and used these skills to make drugs for personal use, as well as a means for financial support.

On August 15, 1979, after having lunch with one of his few friends, Karen Coleman, Dallas disappeared from his Case Hall dorm. Despite the fact that Dallas was still legally a minor, his parents were not informed of his disappearance until four days later.

Case Hall, MSU campus. The college home of James Dallas Egbert III, 2007. *Courtesy of Brad Donaldson.*

When the campus police inspected his dorm room, they discovered evidence of a secret homosexual lifestyle, a mysterious corkboard full of pushpins, and a note that sounded eerily like a suicide note. In this note, Dallas made the request that he be cremated if his body was ever found. Along with the suicide note was found a collection of poems penned by him. One such poem, "Final Destination," might have shed some light into Dallas's mindset in the days leading up to his disappearance. A portion of the poem is as follows:

> "Whenever I decide there's
> A place I'd like to be,
> Soon as I can find there's
> A goal to be achieved.
> Come the time I'm shown that
> There's something left for me,
> Then I'll go, but until then,
> I think I'd rather sleep."

Several theories about Dallas's disappearance surfaced, and the family hired an unorthodox, but successful, private detective named William Dear to help sort out the leads. After reviewing the evidence, several possibilities emerged:

1. Dallas had committed suicide.

2. Dallas had gone into the steam tunnels for another round of Dungeon & Dragons and was killed or injured.

3. Dallas had overdosed on drugs.

4. A homosexual man or group of men was possibly holding Dallas.

5. People who were using his knowledge of how to make drugs were possibly holding Dallas.

6. Dallas might have been murdered.

7. Dallas had a mental breakdown and substituted fantasy for reality. This theory is what started and heightened the urban legend that Dallas could not handle his reality, and slowly became his Dungeons & Dragons character. With this in mind, Dallas was possibly hiding out in a secret room of the steam tunnels.

8. Dallas had been killed or injured while engaging in some dangerous activity; he was after all known to go "trestling" at the railroad tracks running through the MSU campus. Trestling is a game in which you climb on a train trestle, and play "chicken" with an oncoming train. Many MSU students perished from trestling, so it seemed likely he might have met the same horrible fate.

The theory that Dallas was lying injured or dead in the steam tunnels, was quickly dismissed by Michigan State University. The campus insisted that it was not even possible for the tunnels to be entered, despite testimony from several individuals that they enter the tunnels occasionally to play Dungeon & Dragons. Eventually, Detective Dear received permission to enter the tunnels in search of Dallas. He found the tunnels to be extremely dangerous. He did find evidence that Dallas had been down there, but was now gone.

Wanting to use the media in the aid of finding Dallas, but being legally unable to disclose the drug use or Dallas's sexual issues, he decided to play the hand of the Dungeons & Dragons theory with the media. His decision to run with this theory publicly resulted in some unexpected bad side effects. The media picked up the story immediately, sensationalized it, and it led to the damaged image of role-playing games in the public eye.

After much work by Mr. Dear, Dallas was eventually found in New Orleans and the story of his month-long disappearance could finally be told.

Dallas had been planning to disappear for a long time. He had planned to commit suicide on several occasions over the preceding nine-month period. One of the reasons he told his psychologist was the pressure being put on him by his mother, and his fear it would continue for the rest of his life. He expressed an interest in making her suffer in addition to wanting to be free of her.

On August 14, 1979, he put his plans into motion. He had a final lunch with his friend Karen Coleman, went back to Case Hall where he entered the steam tunnels. He took with him a blanket, cartons of milk, some cheese, a few crackers, marijuana, and what he believed to be a large enough quantity of sleeping pills to cause death. Since all urban legend come from some factual beginnings, it is likely that this lead people to believe the rumors that Dallas committed suicide in the tunnels.

When being interviewed by William Dear, Dallas told of his thoughts on that fateful night, "It was clear to me what had to be done. I was depressed and miserable and not even sorry. I should have done it before. Life was no good to me, and this was the best and only solution."

He took all the sleeping pills with the intent of ending his life; he was confused and upset when he awoke the following night. Crawling from the tunnels, he walked a mile to a friend's house.

Dallas having no intentions of being found and knowing the authorities were now looking for him, he enlisted the help of several of his homosexual friends to keep him out of the public eye. Finally, one man, tired of the burden of caring for Dallas, drove him to a bus station and gave him money and a bus ticket to Chicago. He was ordered to use the remaining money for a train ticket to New Orleans. Since Dallas feared this abusive man, he did as he was told.

Dallas started to detoxify while on the train to New Orleans, and could finally think more clearly. His thoughts were still clouded by depression and the intense feeling of rejection, a feeling fueled by the fact that no one really helped him after his suicide attempt.

That night, while staying in a rented hotel room, he purchased the ingredients to make cyanide, mixed the cyanide with a root beer, drank it, and once again waited for death. Once again, he woke up the next day.

Now broke, Dallas had no choice other than to live on the streets of New Orleans. It was here he met a homosexual man from New York. This new friend took him in and convinced Dallas that he should either call his parents or talk with William Dear. He agreed and the mystery surrounding his disappearance ended.

Dallas's relationship with his mother did improve slightly after his return. He got his own small apartment and enrolled at Wright State University. Unfortunately, in early 1980, his depression returned. In April of 1980, Dallas quit college.

On August 11, 1980, four days short of his one-year anniversary of the "steam tunnel incident," James Dallas Egbert III, shot himself in the head in the living room of his apartment. He died at Grandview Hospital five days later, at the age of seventeen.

Dallas's death was nothing short of a tragedy, but the media remained steadfast with their opinions that Dungeons & Dragons played a major role in Dallas's death.

William Dear published his own book called *The Dungeon Master*, and the novel was turned into a made-for-television movie produced in 1982 based off of the Dallas Egbert case called *Mazes and Monsters;* it starred a young Tom Hanks as the main character.

Dallas's ghost is rumored to haunt the steam tunnels under MSU, as well as his apartment near Wayne State. With all the media attention, Dallas will go down in history, especially on the Michigan State University campus, as the "Dungeons & Dragons Death." A child unable to handle reality, but who became a legend.

6

Ransom Eli Olds

While history will show you that Lansing was founded as a real-estate swindle, car fanatics would argue the point. In their eyes, Lansing is R.E. Olds' town.

Ransom Eli Olds (June 3, 1864—August 26, 1950) was a pioneer of the automobile industry. It is well known that he built his first steam car in 1894, and his first gasoline powered car in 1896.

Born in Geneva, Ohio, Ransom was the youngest son of blacksmith Pliny Fiske Olds and his wife, Sarah Whipple Olds. He lived the majority of his childhood years with his family in Cleveland, but eventually settled in Lansing, Michigan, where he married Metta Ursula Woodward on June 5, 1889.

On August 21, 1897, he founded the Olds Motor Vehicle Company in Lansing. In 1899, he sold the business to Samuel L. Smith who changed the company's name to Olds Motor Works and relocated it to the city of Detroit. Ransom remained the Vice President and General Manager of operations. In 1900, Ransom built the first factory made specifically to build motor vehicles, and Oldsmobile was the first to use the assembly line in automotive production 1901. Nevertheless, trouble began to brew for Olds when Samuel's son, Frederick, entered the business. The two men had frequent disagreements that led to Ransom's dismissal from his position in 1904.

This predicament brought Olds back to Lansing where he formed R.E. Olds Motor Car Company. Citing legal concerns over the name with his former company, he renamed his new business the Reo Motor Company. (The REO came from the initials of his name used as an acronym). Olds served as the President, and later, Chairman of REO.

Ransom E. Olds (passenger) in the 1908 REO Roadster, 1936. *Courtesy of Tampa Bay History Center.*

Ransom E. Olds made many other significant contributions to the city of Lansing. He contributed to the success of the Michigan Screw Company and the Atlas Drop Forge Company. He organized the Capital National Bank in 1906, which has since been renamed Lansing Capital Bank and Michigan National Bank. He was also the primary financier of what was and still is the tallest building in Lansing, the Olds Tower. The building, now renamed for its current owners, is best known as the Boji Tower.

R.E.Olds was not only a great businessman, but also a charitable member of society. In fact, when the Engineering building at Michigan State College burned to the ground, he was right there with a donation to build a new one. The building became the R.E. Olds Hall of Engineering and was the first privately-funded building on campus.

In the early 1920s, Ransom began to build what is probably his best known building—the Hotel Olds which was completed in 1926. This building was renamed the George W. Romney Building in 1992, when the State of Michigan decided to use it as the Governor's Office.

With so much of the town's history surrounding him, it is no surprise that the ghostly apparition of R.E. Olds is often reported in many locations around the Lansing area.

The Olds Tomb

Little was ever mentioned of a ghost or haunting in Mount Hope Cemetery prior to the 1990s. The graveyard, located at the northeast corner of Mt. Hope and Aurelius Roads in Lansing, was the final resting place of more than 20,000 people, including many of Lansing's dignitaries. Late in 1991, however, their rest was disturbed by tomb raiders, Richard Kindy and Patrick Wyse.

The mausoleum of the Olds family was broken into and the remains of six of Ransom's relatives were stolen, and thrown into the Grand River; the remains were all recovered, and while no financial ransom was ever asked for, it seems that Ransom, himself, may be just what they received. It was shortly after this theft, that visitors began to report seeing a man who resembled Mr. Olds, near the family's crypt at all hours of the night.

One local paranormal investigator told me, "They really don't let us in there at night, but sometimes we risk it anyways. I for one know of three or four people who have seen him first hand. I even have a picture I would be happy to show you."

The investigator never produced this evidence to me, but I do not doubt that the desecration of his family's tomb could have caused Ransom Olds to turn sentry at a mausoleum.

While interviewing another of the "witnesses," I was told, "When we approached the grand cement stairway leading to the family tomb, we were intercepted by a figure I can only call Mr. Olds." She continued, "I let him know we meant no harm to him or his family, and were only interested in solving the family mystery. He then allowed us to pass. When I stared into the frosted windows, I was suddenly filled with a feeling of grief for the loss experienced by Mr. Olds. I can't even imagine what I would feel like if someone stole the bodies of my loved ones."

R.E. Olds Transportation Museum

In 2003, when I first visited Lansing, I had only one must-see location on my list, the R.E. Olds Transportation Museum. The quaint museum was formerly a Capital Area Transportation Authority garage and was opened in 1981 to highlight Lansing's automobile history.

Olds Family mausoleum, Mt. Hope Cemetery, 2007. *Courtesy of Brad Donaldson.*

When you first approach this one-time bustling garage, you would never guess it is reportedly home to several spirits, including Ransom Olds.

Initially, the thought this building might be haunted never entered my mind, I was there only to see my beloved Oldsmobiles, fate it seems intervened. As I was admiring the 1970 Olds 442, the gift shop clerk approached me. He had been dying to tell someone of his experiences in the building and after noticing my WPARanormal Investigations T-shirt thought I might just be the right man to listen.

He began by telling of the day he was sweeping up near the 1932 Reo hearse/ambulance when he noticed someone had snuck in the back, apparently to enjoy a private, after-hours tour of the premises.

"I quickly realized I was the only one in the building and started to panic; there was no security guard on duty, and as you can see I am a small man." He continued, "I slowly made my way toward the phone in the gift shop area. It was then that I realized there was no on in there, and in fact the doors never opened, I figured I must have had imagined it all."

I continued to listen, relatively sure I knew what was coming next, yet still hanging on every word, he went on to say:

"Each night as I helped to clean up, I made a point to look toward this car, it became very common for me to see a variety of people around it, none of them ever really seemed dead or ghostlike, but it was obvious that is what they indeed were."

I was thrilled to hear this and wanted to run back to the vehicle that I had previously ignored. He sensed my excitement and continued:

"You know if you want to go check out that car, I will be glad to wait here. When you get back I will tell you where I have seen Ransom himself."

This offer froze me in my tracks, there was no way I was going anywhere other than to that spot; I just had to wait for him to let me know where that spot was.

"Ransom is often seen around the corner in that glass room; it is sealed and climate controlled. The alarm never goes off so I am sure it is him, besides if you were dead wouldn't you want to be near the oldest example of your legacy?"

Oddly enough, I was puzzled by what he meant by the oldest example of his legacy more than I was intrigued by the haunting. It turned out the car Ransom is often reported to be looking at was the famous 1897 Olds Motor Works car, the oldest intact automobile in the world, a car on loan from the Smithsonian.

I rushed toward this vehicle in awe of its craftsmanship, longing to be able to touch it, I now knew if I were R.E. Olds, this is exactly where I would be.

When I started to work on this chapter, I tried to contact this employee, but was informed he no longer worked in the museum. Luckily, I received an e-mail from the same man through our Web site; he was submitting these stories along with one more. This next story makes me wonder if he is stalking the ghost of R.E. Olds or if the ghost is following him.

"I often missed my visits with Mr. Olds, and was drawn to investigate his life in even more depth; I traveled to Ann Arbor, to visit his former home, which is now open for public tours. When I was in the master bath, I was once again face-to-face with this behemoth of the automobile industry; I was humbled and yet scared. I left and drove straight home from Ann Arbor to Lansing faster than the Spartan Football Team leaving after a humiliating defeat to U of M."

I have made many visits to Lansing in the past year, but have yet to make it back to this Mecca of the automobile industry. I have been distracted visiting other haunted sites, gathering evidence and photographs of other haunted locations in this wonderful town. I do hope to one day visit the museum again, and if the stars are lined up properly, maybe I too will be able to be face-to-face with this man— I, however, would not run. I would most likely break out my digital recorder and attempt to record a radio show segment, or at least some stellar EVP.

7
Lansing's
Haunted Homes

Have you ever driven down a residential neighborhood and wondered if any of the houses were haunted? I know, as a child, I would go past the old creepy-looking houses in Ionia, Michigan, and imagine that they held ghosts that would walk through the halls at night and peek at us through the windows.

One thing that I have learned since childhood was that a house does not have to look spooky to be haunted. Nor is it a requirement that there be a death in the house in order for it to be haunted. Residents of newer homes have reported anywhere from moderate paranormal activity to sometimes frightening unexplainable experiences.

Britten Manor, 2007.
Courtesy of Brad Donaldson.

Many paranormal investigators and researchers have speculated as to the explanation of why a house would be haunted. Some theorize that the entities do not realize that they are dead, while other theories include that the spirit is "stuck" at the location if they were the victim of a murder or suicide. It is also believed by some that a haunted house is nothing more than the spirits of passed loved ones visiting the living and that the haunting has nothing to do with the property itself.

Whatever might have caused the haunting, we have included many haunted houses to choose from. The following pages are some of the haunted homes in and around the Lansing area. These homes may look normal from the outside, but are anything but normal on the inside.

Britten Manor

The house on Britten Avenue looks like an ordinary home, perfectly normal to anyone passing by—at least from the outside. Inside, the house holds a friendly entity.

Formerly known as Britten Manor, an adult foster care home, residents have claimed to look forward to their ghostly experiences with the female spirit. The Former owners, Kenneth and Delores Goff, enjoyed their paranormal experiences in this home and will always treasure those memories.

The entity in question is believed to be the wife of William Britten. In 1922, the Brittens moved into their new house to settle in for a happy life. All that tragically changed in May of 1923, when Mrs. Britten was killed on the brand new stairway. Research on the property showed a Mr. William Britten and Mrs. Pearl Britten both lived in the new home in 1922. According to the City Directories of Lansing in 1923, Pearl was removed from the listing as a current tenant of the home, only her husband was listed. The 1924 City Directory also showed that William, probably out of grief over his wife's murder, had moved away from the house at 706 Britten and settled into a new home in Lansing.

Workers and elderly residents of the former manor believe that Pearl still walks the halls. A news story dated on October 31, 1997 quoted Delores Goff as saying, "Most of our residents believe that she is here. It is nothing concrete. We just all believe it. One of the residents say that she (Pearl) would come up and pat her on the shoulder."

Delores herself claimed that she had experienced paranormal activity several times. She stated that many times she has heard a woman's voice calling her name. "I get up and there's nobody there," Delores says. "Everybody is in bed. It's all quiet."

The Goffs no longer own the Britten Manor. The adult foster care facility has a new owner and has been renamed Evergreen Place. Regardless of the new operators and name, Pearl probably still makes her rounds of the building, calling out residents' names.

Hillsdale Street

Running parallel to West St. Joseph Street to the north sits Hillsdale Street. When Rick C. bought his 1910 house, he never imagined that he would be buying a haunted house. However, in 1994, one of Rick's friends may have convinced him otherwise.

Rick's friend, a security guard, visited the home and knew that something was wrong in the home. During a moment of pure instinct, and to the surprise of Rick, the friend pulled his revolver and aimed it into a bedroom. Rick looked into the bedroom, expecting to view something of a frightening nature, and was equally surprised to find the room empty. His friend was anything but calm.

"Why didn't you tell me about her?" his friend had asked. Rick was obviously confused by the reference of a female that no one knew about or could see. Upon questioning, Rick's friend described seeing an unknown female who was tall, wearing a long black dress and a black bonnet with white lace. Upon his description of the female apparition, his friend theorized the period of the clothing to be from the 1800s.

Rick then recalled several instances of the floor creaking in the hallway, as if someone was walking across it. Upon trying to debunk the sounds, the floor would not creak when a human would walk the same area. As Rick describes it, "these are not the normal noises the house makes when it's settling."

Rick decided to do a little research on the property and found a map of Lansing in the 1860s. This map clearly showed that a house once stood on the property, and this was not the home that he was currently living in.

"I think it's a friendly entity, one who looks out for us," Rick stated in a *Lansing State Journal* article. "That's why it roams the halls, keeping a check on us."

Park Lane House

"Eve." That was the name spelled out on an Ouija board during a séance. We may never know exactly who Eve was and why her spirit remains in a house on Park Lane, but several residents of the home will tell you that Eve makes her presence well known.

Former resident Andrea Kress and her roommates were the ones who held the séance, to attempt to communicate with the entity and validate some of the strange occurrences that were taking place on a continuous basis.

Andrea and her roommates would be disturbed by unexplained loud knocking noises. Footsteps throughout the house could be heard when no one else was home, as well as banging from the attic. Andrea claimed that it sounded like "someone jumping up and down in the attic."

These unexplained occurrences are what prompted Andrea and her roommates to partake in a séance, using a Ouija board. They wanted to know if this activity was product of a ghost or of their own productive imaginations. To them, the name "Eve" became a validation.

Upon leaving the Park Lane house, Andrea wondered if the new tenants would also come to know "Eve" and if the activity would continue for them.

Andrea was correct. "Eve" would continue her mischievous forays with the new tenants.

For Colleen McKinnie, it all started a week after she moved into the Park Lane house. She found it strange that all of her hair accessories and products were disappearing. Obviously, Colleen would have asked her roommates about the missing items, probably under the assumption that one of her roommates were borrowing her items and forgetting to return them. It became apparent that something else was happening when her other roommates were also having items disappearing, such as their perfumes.

"We'd gone out, locked our doors, and our stuff was gone the next morning," said Colleen. "We've also been here when we noticed our stuff missing. We tried talking to the entity; we would ask for our stuff back, but it did not work. "

The ominous knocking and banging noises continued for the new tenants. Instead of the attic, their knocking noises were emanating from the front, back, and basement doors. "You'll open the door and no one will be there," Colleen stated. "You'll shut the door, walk away, and you'll hear it again. But nobody's near."

Not only were knocking noises coming from the doors, but the bathroom door was prone to randomly flying open and slamming shut. Alarm clocks being turned off or reset was a constant annoyance that was attributed to "Eve."

Another roommate had a frightening experience in the Park Lane house. Resident Jennie Wagner, smoking in one of the rooms in the house, placed the cigarette butt in the ashtray and left the room. Upon re-entering the room, the ashtray was on fire. Was the mischievous "Eve" beginning to make her presence known in ways that are more malevolent?

Jennie has the perfect response for anyone who is skeptical of his or her experiences and refuses to believe in the possibility of a haunting on Park Lane.

"You can't logically explain it. But for five separate people to experience things on different occasions and for people who have lived here before to experience similar things, rules out the possibility that we are all crazy."

The Smoking House

Paranormal investigators theorize that renovations and construction of any kind within a building or home can cause paranormal activity to either begin or heighten. Our research with clients tends to show exactly that. One business in Grand Rapids never had a "paranormal problem" until they knocked down an original basement wall and opened up the other side for storage use. By the time this business owner contacted us, it was a paranormal smorgasbord of activity!

Renovations of a new home is believed to have prompted this next haunting to take place.

On New Year's Eve, in the 1960s, a fire broke out in the Parisian home, killing both parents and their young teenage son. Shortly thereafter, a new family of five purchased the home. The father took it upon himself to renovate the burnt-out structure, and accomplished this while also working full time for the City of Lansing. It was during the reconstruction that several strange events took place. Some of these events were later witnessed by one or all of the family members.

The first encounters occurred during the renovation process. While Bill, the father, was working on the house, he was constantly interrupted by a tapping on his shoulder. Each time Bill would turn around to come face-to-face with a middle-aged woman. This silent apparition would stand there looking at Bill, and then would vanish suddenly in front of his eyes. On one occasion, Bill tried to communicate to the entity, but with no success. The woman would continue to stand there silently and then disappear. Bill told only his wife of these experiences.

When the family was finally able to move into their new home, they never dreamt that they would be departing the premises only twelve months later.

One Sunday morning, the middle child, Doris, decided to stay home from church due to feeling ill. Doris was in the kitchen when she peered into the living room to see whom she thought was her eldest sister, Elizabeth, standing in the room. Elizabeth did not answer her when she questioned why she had arrived home early from church. Upon nothing but silence coming from the living room, Doris went to check on Elizabeth, only to her astonishment, she found a boy standing in the living room. The young man looked to be in his teens with dark hair, blue eyes, and wearing jeans and a sweatshirt. Frightened, all Doris could do was stand there and stare at the boy, who then vanished before her eyes. Doris immediately ran out of the house and reserved herself to wait outside until her family's return. Doris, confused and unsure about what she just witnessed, did not tell her mother about this experience until after the family moved from the home.

The youngest child, Carol, also had her own strange experience. On this day, Carol was home alone when she walked up the stairs to the bedrooms and was startled to see someone standing in the bathroom. Within seconds, it became clear that the figure in the bathroom was a teenage boy, standing quietly and looking into the bathroom mirror. The entity became aware of Carol's presence and turned from the mirror to face her directly. Carol estimated that she was approximately fifteen feet away from the boy at this point.

The boy's eyes met with Carol's for a brief moment before the boy suddenly vanished. Carol, deeply troubled by this event, only communicated it to her mother.

Later, the family learned that the second floor bathroom is the location of the teenage son's death in that fatal fire.

Strange events continued in the home, even involving the family dog. The dog, normally an abnormally quiet animal, seemed to be uncomfortable in the new house. He would frequently bark for unexplained reasons and was constantly restless. On one particular day, he leapt from an open window of their second story bathroom, onto the cement driveway below. The dog was not killed, but was in fact quite dazed when the family found him. Upon inspection of the bathroom, paw prints were found on the freshly painted windowsill and they were able to piece together the story of how the dog came to lay in their driveway.

Bill, suspicious of the activity in the home and with the knowledge of the deaths that occurred, was reluctant to view any pictures of the previous residents of the home. However, eventually a neighbor showed him a photograph of Mr. and Mrs. Parisian. As he secretly suspected, he was able to identify positively the wife as the lady that had interrupted his work by constantly tapping on his shoulder.

More research ensued and it was quickly discovered that the girls attended the same school as the teenage boy who perished in the home. Carol and Doris later came across a class photo of the Parisian boy. Even though no one could be positive it was the same person, there was a striking resemblance between the photo and the young boy that was seen in their home.

At no time did the family see the husband in the home. Equally unusual is that Elizabeth never witnessed anything strange. While at no time did the family feel threatened by the unseen residents, they decided twelve months later that they must leave. However, before the moving process was completed, one final occurrence took place.

Carol and her father went alone to retrieve a few last remaining items in the home. Upon pulling into the driveway, both of them saw smoke emanating upward from the newly completed surface of the roof. Bill told Carol to stay in the vehicle while he went inside the house to investigate. He emerged some time later without identifying the source of the smoke. Simultaneously, a neighbor ran out from one of their homes and yelled, "Bill, it looks like it's on fire again!" This time the neighbor and Bill went inside and investigated the house for the source. Just as before, they emerged from the house with no evidence as to the cause of this mysterious smoke. Bill and the neighbor decided to vacate the property. Bill hastily grabbed the last remaining items from the house and they quickly departed.

Occasionally, when the family returns to Lansing, they drive past their former home and remember their experiences. Majority of the time, the home would have a "For Sale" sign posted in the front yard.

Down On the Farm

Just south of the State's Capitol rests a community that radiates small town charm—but they also experience a small town haunting.

On the outskirts of this quaint little town, rests a typical farmhouse with a father, a mother, three children, and at least two not-so-typical residents. Life on the farm for this family was normal and quiet for decades until ten years ago; that all changed. They have no idea why it began or who it is that now haunts their once peaceful home.

The first indication of something brewing was when the father was coming home from the bank. Upon pulling into the driveway, he saw someone standing just inside the door of the barn. When he headed over to the barn to have a look, no one was there.

A few weeks later, a friend of the family stopped by for a visit; the husband went out to greet his friend when he arrived. His friend stopped suddenly for a second or two after vacating his pickup and stared up at the barn. After some questioning, his friend told of seeing a man standing just outside the barn door. The friend described a man that looked to be in his sixties wearing bib overalls and a baseball cap. The husband was amazed. The description perfectly matched the gentleman he saw weeks before standing at the doorway of the barn.

Apparently, the entity that haunts the barn seems benevolent. At one point or another, two of the children have witnessed this man and even the family dog responds with friendly wagging at something unseen in the barn. One day, the children saw the man standing near the barn as they got off the school bus during a winter afternoon. Even though the father never talked to the children about this mysterious man, both children's descriptions matched the gentleman the father and his friend had seen. Inspection of the snow in and around the barn produced no footprints.

Soon the male entity would have a female companion. The first to encounter this new resident was the wife. After baking pies for supper, she went outside to retrieve the mail. Upon closing the door, she heard the lock activate and she just knew that she was locked out of the house. Even though she knew her attempt was going to be in vain, she tried to open the door anyway. Giving up, she started to walk back down the porch when she heard the distinct sound of her door unlocking and then swinging open. She immediately ran up the porch and into the living room where she was shocked to see a woman going up the stairs. Being too frightened to follow this entity to the second floor, she returned to the kitchen to find yet another surprise. All the pies were now out of the oven and cooling off on the countertop.

A few weeks after the "pie episode," the kids had their own experience with the female ghost. One day, the youngest of the children was preparing the tub for a bath. Leaving the tap running, he went back into this room. The oldest child, hearing the water constantly running, decided to march upstairs to confront her brother and turn the water off before it overflowed. As she approached her brother in his room and started to yell at him, she heard the water being turned off. Sure that her mother must have also been worried about the tub overflowing, she glanced inside the bathroom only to find the room empty and her confusion growing. As she turned away from the bathroom, she spotted the blurry figure of a woman descending the staircase. After conversing with her mother, it was understood that they both saw the same female entity. They described their new houseguest as being in her late fifties, maybe early sixties, with dark hair and a blue dress.

The family can only speculate if the male and female entities are actually husband and wife. That is one mystery that will likely never be solved, but the family has gotten used to their new "hired farm-hands."

The Webberville House

Webberville, Michigan, is a small farming community just south-east of Lansing. This claimed haunted house sits only a mere ten miles away from the infamous Seven Gables Road legend.

The two-story single-family home was built in 1866, and is surround-ed by farmland and large expansions of woods just off to the north.

The "Blake" family moved into their home and never felt quite comfortable. Later, family members would admit to one another the eerie feelings that permeated the home and the overbearing feeling that there was an unseen presence continuously watching them.

The sounds of footsteps coming down the stairs were a constant sound that the family got used to, but the sound of a young girl's voice resonating from the second story unnerved them. No matter how many times they would look to see if someone was upstairs, the voiced could never be recognized or explained away.

A member of the Blake family went on to explain the most disturbing incident that took place while residing in the home. One evening, the family went out to dinner, only to return to find their washer and dryer now sitting in the kitchen. No signs of a break in could be found to explain the movement of the appliances. Another clue that was odd to the family was the lack of marks on the floor to show the evidence of where the appliances had been dragged.

The family decided to redecorate some of the upstairs rooms. Upon tearing down the wallpaper in one of the bedroom, they discovered charcoal drawings covering the walls. Even though the family member did not describe what the drawings were, he commented that they were noticeably old and that it was an original wall. The family will often wonder if these 1800s charcoal sketching holds any connection to the young girl's spirit that seems trapped in the one of the upstairs bedrooms.

Ghost Girl

Residing quieting in a colonial two-story home is a family of four with a disturbing secret. Many people would claim the residents to be weird and "out of their minds," but the family, especially the mother, we will call Lisa, feels that she has the spirit of a little girl that is clinging to her side.

The home, built in 1938, sits in the middle of a much older section of Lansing. The historic housing community established in 1890s included a nearby church. Records indicated that the church once owned Lisa's home and rented it out. There are also unconfirmed suspicions that there may have been another building where Lisa's house now stands.

Lisa has encountered the apparition of a small girl many times at the top of the staircase. What is puzzling is the lack of sightings of this young child by anyone else in the family, nor the sightings taking place anywhere else in the house. Lisa often wonders who this child is and why she only appears to her, and in the same spot, when Lisa stands near the bottom of the stairs.

On one occasion, Lisa had the opportunity to visit with a person who deals with aura photography. The results astounded Lisa and helped her suspicions that the spirit of the young girl could be following her. It was determined that Lisa had two auras—one was her own and the other was a small child physically close to her.

Lisa eventually called in a local paranormal team, the Ghost Research Centre, to help explain the child apparition that only she could see.

Immediately, the paranormal team determined that there was a high EMF (electromagnetic field) level running through parts of the living room and at the foot of the stairs. Strong magnetic fields can have adverse affects on humans. High EMF levels have been attributed to causing nausea, headaches, and arrhythmia. What interests paranormal investigators is that strong levels can also cause paranoia (feelings of being watched) and hallucinations. So, could this be the cause of the ghostly entity? Perhaps Lisa, being sensitive to high magnetic levels, only thinks she is seeing a young girl, when nothing actually exists. This could explain why no other family member has witnessed this ghostly visitor.

Even though evidence from the paranormal investigation did not confirm or debunk the child spirit that seemingly resides at the top of the stairs, it did find another possible entity in the home. Earlier in the day, the lead investigator was recording Lisa's tour of the house with a digital audio recorder. Upon analysis of the recording, the investigators stumbled upon some surprising evidence. Apparently, a male entity was present in the home and followed them throughout the tour of the house, making comments as the tour was progressing along. Several EVPs (Electronic Voice Phenomena) were captured in the home, mostly in the sunroom. One EVP captured the attention of the investigators in particular. It was the disembodied male voice declaring a name, "Elsie," and possibly confirming that a female spirit just may be residing in the home after all.

The Stoddard Street Ghost

This eerie story was submitted by a former MSU student who was renting a house on Stoddard Street with four other male MSU students. The two-story house can be found between Albert and Frye Streets.

This former resident, named "Bill," talked about his first experience with the supernatural.

"One evening while sleeping in the upstairs bedroom, I awoke to the sound of labored breathing, as if someone was choking. The sound seemed to be emanating from the outside. Figuring it was one of my roommates playing a joke on me, I slowly approached the window, expecting to catch the perpetrator standing on the roof outside my bedroom window. When I got to the window I could not see anyone standing on the roof, but the sound of the gasping breath was just as audible. I began to get angry so I opened up my bedroom door and yelled loud enough to wake my four roommates that I wanted the games to stop so I can sleep."

The four roommates staggered half-asleep from their rooms wondering what Bill's problem was. Bill told them about the noise, and that it could still be heard coming from his room. The roommates, all believing that Bill was suffering from nothing more than a weird dream, walked into his room to investigate this alleged noise. With a level of surprise, the remaining roommates could hear it, too. Looking at one another in astonishment, they completely investigated the room to find the source of this "breathing," including venturing outside and walking around the perimeter of the house. Nothing to explain the noise was ever discovered and the sound dissipated about an hour later. The roommates returned to their beds but none of them got any sleep for the remainder of the night.

A couple of weeks later, everyone in the house went home for the weekend, except for one of the roommates, "Allen." Allen had stayed out late on Friday night, attending a party before heading out to work the next day.

After a long day at work, Allen returned to the house to catch up on the much-needed sleep he'd deprived himself the night before. He telephoned a friend he was to meet later and told the gentleman to stop by and wake him up around seven o'clock, so he would have plenty of time to get ready for a night out at a local bar. Allen also told his friend that he would leave the front door unlocked so the guy could get into the house.

Allen soon fell asleep and he estimated that he was sleeping for about four to five hours when he was awakened by the sound of the front screen door creaking open and then slamming shut. Thinking it was his friend arriving to wake him up, but still feeling extremely exhausted, Allen remained in bed. He could hear the sounds of his friend's footsteps throughout the house and walking up the staircase. Listening to the sounds, Allen could clearly hear the footsteps stop at the landing at the top of the stairs, pause, and then continue toward his bedroom door. Still very tired, he heard his bedroom door open, someone entering the room, approaches the bed, and sat down on the corner of his mattress.

In a sleepy haze, Allen rolled over to talk to his friend and was shocked to discover that no one was there. Even more of a shock was Allen noticing that his blankets still had an imprint of someone sitting on the edge of the bed, and he could still feel the weight. Allen grabbed his pants and quickly left the room.

When seven o'clock arrived, his friend was surprised to find Allen sitting on the couch in the living room. After explaining to his buddy what just happened in his room, and adding the story of what transpired a couple of weeks prior, Allen was starting to believe that a supernatural being possibly was residing among them in the house. His friend sympathized as best he could, but had no logical reasons for the two events. Still puzzled and now a little scared, Allen returned to his room, dressed for the evening out, and left the house.

The roommates started to notice other odd occurrences in the house, such as things disappearing, doors opening and closing, the sounds of eerie footsteps roaming the house, and even a few repeat performances of the "breathing" previously heard, always in Bill's room. No logical reason for any of the activity could be found.

Eventually, the roommates graduated from MSU and went their separate ways. However, you can be sure that all of them still hold onto memories of their experiences with the paranormal.

Ghostly Frolicking
at the Frat House

Fraternity houses are always well known for parties and girlfriends spending the night. One MSU frat house also seems to have parties where only the unseen entities are invited.

Alex was sleeping on his futon bed that was situated on the floor underneath his roommate's loft, with a small curtain draping down for privacy. Laying beside him on the futon was his girlfriend, Katherine. After dozing for quite some time, Alex was awakened by the sound of Alex's roommate, Dave, climbing the stairs to the loft and getting into bed. With the bed shaking and moving, Katherine abruptly awoke and asked Alex what the commotion was. Alex simply explained that it was Dave getting into bed and encouraged her to go back to sleep.

Only mere seconds after Alex whispered to Katherine and laid his head back on the pillow, the door to the room opened and yet again the couple heard and felt someone else climb up the stairs and roll around in the loft above.

Now out of curiosity of whom Dave convinced to sleep with him, Alex pulled his head out from under the drapes to ask teasingly of Dave if he would like some privacy. Dave replied that he did not have anyone in the bed with him and he was confused why Alex was asking him such "a dumb question."

"I told him what my girlfriend and I'd just heard. After hearing our story, Dave said that when he came to bed, no one was in his bed. "Needless to say, all of us were a little freaked out."

Putting this unexplained event in the back of his mind he went about his normal college life until a few weeks later, he once again had an encounter with the paranormal.

Alex was pulling an all-night study session with another resident in the main formal room of the fraternity house. At approximately five o'clock in the morning, Alex and his study partner was interrupted by the sound of the old creaky door to the stairway opening and heard someone walking into the foyer, which was the room next to the formal room. Expecting to hear one of their friends complaining about being awakened, Alex asked aloud who was there. Upon asking the question, the footsteps immediately stopped and no one responded from the next room. With his curiosity extremely piqued, Alex and his friend got up from their seats and walked into the foyer. No one was there!

A few second later, however, the two friends witnessed something that they will never forget.

"I saw a shadow of a person," stated Alex. "It moved on the wall as if the person was walking away. However, the footsteps ceased while the shadow kept moving. This was a very distinct shadow."

What is Alex's statement on how he felt about his foray with a paranormal being?

"It freaked me out pretty heavily."

The Lost Boy

The former site of a Native American tribe and messing around with Ouija boards is not a good combination. One young man in East Lansing was taught just that lesson.

Brad always suspected that there was something "not right" about the house.

"I didn't even like walking between the houses and parking area," he explained. "Although it was only a normal house along a dirt road in the country, it was totally creepy!"

Brad and several other friends would write and record music in their makeshift studio they'd built in the basement. Soon, paranormal activity began that justified his eerie feelings. Unexplained power surges were becoming commonplace among their time spent in the basement. Several times while recording, the studio would suddenly become numbingly cold, with the phenomena lasting for sometimes up to five minutes, only to dissipate, allowing the young people to warm back up. Knocking and rapping noises were starting to become a constant nuisance in the studio.

One night, while Brad and a friend were in the kitchen getting a snack, he witnessed something he could not explain in his peripheral vision. The dark figure "ran" from the basement stairs, through the dining room area and into the living room. Thinking that he was possibly seeing a cat, he asked his friend if he saw the figure as well. His friend, feeling just as shocked as Brad, confirmed that he saw what appeared to be a "dark gray blob, floating about six inches off the floor."

"I knew then that we both saw the same thing!" Brad exclaimed.

When the two friends went to the basement door, it was shut. Because of this discovery, they decided to continue to experiment with what they both knew was a short event with the paranormal.

Armed with a homemade compass, they walked around the house to confirm that the magnetic needle was always pointing north. When they were satisfied that their compass would give an accurate reading, they walked the "gray blob's" path through the house. With surprise, the compass would spin continuously counterclockwise. As soon as the boys would leave the area, the compass would point back to north.

Later that night, after a 2 a.m. Taco Bell run, Brad's friend suggested they create a homemade Ouija board in an attempt to communicate with the entity that they knew was residing in the house. Using a white board from the basement studio and messing up the lettering on the board, Brad and his friend sat down on the floor, on the spot where their compass did a fanatical dance. Using their compass as a planchett, they moved their instrument in a figure eight motion while asking their new "houseguest" several questions.

Almost immediately, the pair began to receive a response. After several more inquiries, they learned that the entity was the spirit of a young boy whom claimed to be lost and confused. With further questioning as to who he was looking for, the compass needle spelled out the letters M-A-M-A.

At this point, Brad became extremely upset and decided to not only end their Ouija board experiment, but that he needed to leave the house altogether. In addition, he did so, with amazing swiftness.

"I've never liked being in that house since then, but at least we knew who was messing with us," said Brad. "Needless to say, we never tried it again. I was pretty freaked out."

Cravens Mills

In 1836, the Craven Family made the long and tiresome journey utilizing only Indian trails, as no roads existed at that time, from Delaware County, Ohio. Upon reaching their destination, the Craven's established the first settlement approximately three quarters of a mile from the present village of Elsie, Michigan. At the time of the Craven settlement, this region was a vast wilderness inhabited by the Saginaw Chippewa Indians. Luckily, these Indians were friendly and the children of the early settlers often played with the native Indian children.

In hopes of becoming a thriving settlement, Robert Craven constructed two sawmills and a dam that spread between several Craven Family farms. Soon after the Craven's arrival, seventeen more families settled in "Cravens Mills," the original name given to the village. On June 18, 1857, Cravens Mill was renamed Elsie, in honor of the first child to be born in this new village, Elsie Tillotson.

Throughout the 172-year history of Elsie and its surrounding areas, portions of the original farms were split into parcels and sold off for new housing developments and modern farms.

Through property research, Lori's property is an original segment of a former Cravens Mills farm. Lori also lives in a section amusingly named "Lightning Alley," where strange electrical phenomena occur often. Present is a stray voltage in the ground that has shocked the livestock at the watering tank. The property is also prone to unusually high amounts of lightning strikes. Consumers Energy could not figure out where the power leakage that was affecting the animals was originating from, but they did place a device on the breaker box to allow the lightning to disperse without doing damage to the house.

If this was not unusual enough, Lori started to suspect that her house might also hold unseen residents. While out working with her livestock, Lori would hear someone running up to her, yell something in her ear, and then run away. Looking around, there would never be anyone present. Majority of the time, she cannot make out the words that are being spoken to her by a male voice. One day, she was startled to hear a female voice as well. Unnerved by the phenomena happening around her, she called in paranormal investigators to help explain some of the occurrences.

Joseph Stewart and former member Kim from the Ghost Research Centre answered Lori's call for help. The investigation began between the barns where a great deal of the paranormal activity occured. While walking the property, Lori jumped and yelled out, "See, I just got buzzed again!" Surprised, Joe and Kim quickly did an EMF sweep of the area. Nothing unusual could be detected. However, later it was discovered on digital audio, that an EVP (electronic voice phenomena) of a man talking, followed by a female and a child's voice was captured at the moment when Lori stated that she was being "buzzed."

Numerous other EVPs were also captured during this investigation, but very few of the EVPs captured was from inside of the house. The area between the barns, along with the pasture, looks as if it is the favorite location for these spirits of the dead to communicate with the living.

The Ghost Research Centre plans to return to this location to further their investigation into the haunted claims of Cravens Mills.

"My Experiences with the Ghost"

This testimony was sent to me by the Ghost Research Centre concerning a former case. After receiving this document, I was preparing to review the story to see how I would write it up for this chapter. Instead, I elected to allow the story to remain, as is, a true testimony of one family's experience with the supernatural. I have deleted the actual address of the home, and omitted majority of all names.

"I will briefly detail some of my experiences with ghosts, while I was living on the south side of Lansing, Michigan. I will begin with a brief statement of the history of the house. This residence was built by General Motors Corporation in 1928, and was intended for the use of those of their employees who had to travel. Not much is known of those who resided in the house over the years. I do know that the owner previous to me was a lady named Marie Stebbins, who sold the house in 1945. Until my husband and I bought it in 1982, the house was rented out to various people. We know very little about Marie's history: for example, we are not sure if this is the same person as a lady with the same name who once took a sea voyage to Europe. But, we do know one fact about her psychology from the deed to the house: she seems to have had racist tendencies, since she forbids the sale of the house to those of African American descent. This fact about Marie seems to have found confirmation in one of the EVP results obtained by ghost hunter Joseph Stewart in the house in 2007. In this recording, Marie appears to make a racial slur directed to one of the neighbors, who is a gentleman from Costa Rica. Indeed, investigator Stewart takes this to be an independent corroboration of the veracity of these recordings, since he himself did not know of Marie's racism at the time of the recording.

Before giving my experiences, it might be well to briefly describe the house. My husband and I bought the house in 1982, after renting it for six months. It is a very small, single-level dwelling, with a crawl space instead of a basement, and no garage. It does, however, have an acre of land behind it, including a small wooded area. And, it does have a small, rustic-style deck attached to the house out back. When it was built in 1928, it was only 400 square feet, but over the years, it was renovated three times. Thus, when we bought it in 1982 it had about 800 square feet. It is an oddly shaped house, rather resembling a Halloween face. There are only three bedrooms, a small kitchen and bathroom, and somewhat larger living room. The room where most of the ghostly happenings have occurred is the bedroom facing east, which we call the "green room." As you will see from the following narrative, however, the ghosts sometimes appear in other areas of the house, such as in the hallway between the green room and the bedroom facing west (which we call the "red room").

I will now turn to my experiences in the house. From the beginning, something attracted me to the house. I felt that I was supposed to be there: Indeed, I even felt that the house would never let me go, and that I was destined to die in it. I also felt that there was a conscious presence in the house, and that whoever (or whatever) it was wanted to look after me and protect me. Indeed, after divorcing my husband in 1987, I often felt that this unknown presence wanted

to protect me from some of the alcoholic men with whom, unfortunately, I became associated. It is not that the ghosts ever physically
intervened to protect me: Nevertheless, I often felt that they made
me stronger inside, so that I could stand up for myself and fight
back. These feelings of a presence were always a bit nebulous, but it
seemed to me to be a woman's presence. (As we will see, however,
my grandson also felt a presence, but in his case, it was always a
man that he felt!) One more point about these feelings: Toward the
end of my residency (I moved out in December, 2006), I began to feel
more afraid of the house. I felt that the presence did not want to let
me go, and even felt that the presence might be angry with me.

I was not the only one to feel these vague feelings. My son was
very scared of sleeping in the green room (this was in 1988, when
he was eight years old). Part of the reason for this might have been
connected to the fact that my husband had discovered some odd
things when checking the crawl space under the house. He came
across a water heater, an old wood door, and a strange mound
covered with plastic that seemed to resemble a grave. This mound
was directly under the green room: Thus, the running joke in our
family was that there was a grave under Mike's room! I suppose
this might have affected Mike's imagination, but it is worth noting
that to this day Mike is deathly afraid of being alone in that room. In
addition to this, during the years 2002 through 2003 my grandson
(who was ten years old at the time) often felt the presence of a man
in the house. These experiences occurred when he would come to
sleep over, mostly during the summer months. He never wanted to
sleep in the green room, but instead always slept in the living room. I
came to find out that this was because he could feel the presence of
a man in that room. I also found out (in 2006) that he had sometimes
experienced "cold spots" in the hallway.

I will now turn to some more concrete experiences. Sometime
in the fall of 1991, my second husband and I were home during the
afternoon. I was in the bathroom with the door open, and he was

in the kitchen, when both of us heard the side door slam (this door leads outside from the dining room). The door had not even been open at the time. I could see my husband go to investigate, but he stopped short before reaching the door. He told me that he had felt something very cold pass by him toward the door. He was not the kind of person to admit to any fear, but I could see that he was shaken; he was as white as a ghost!

In the year 2000, I was finally divorced again, and I did not have another relationship until I met my present husband in December, 2003. From that time on, I felt that the presence was glad that I was finally alone. Although I felt that the presence wanted me to live in the house alone, nothing strange ever happened to my husband when he visited me at the house. (In fact, my husband remains very skeptical about the existence of ghosts: he tells me that although he often stayed awake late at night reading, he never felt any unseen presences or "cold spots.") For my part, however, I often heard people talking in low voices at various points in the house (during the years 2003 to 2006), and sometimes encountered gray shadows at night just before going to bed. On one occasion (I think it was in the spring of 2006), I observed the shadow of a very short person pass by in the hallway (I was sitting in bed at the time, in the bedroom next to the green room, and the shadow had come from the direction of the green room). I was fully awake at the time, and could see clearly that it was the shadow of a man with broad shoulders, wearing a top hat. The shadow also was very short: Either it was a very small person, or else it was walking below the level of the floor.

After 2004, I was taking night classes at Lansing Community College, so I frequently got home at 10:30 pm. I would always enter the house from the side door, and frequently I felt that someone was there when I entered. I also began to experience cold spots around the house: Most of these were experienced in the hallway between the green room and red room, and in a little space off the hallway (where a wash machine had once stood). In addition to these experiences, I would sometimes hear knocking at the front door late at night. When I would investigate, I always found that no one was there. On one occasion (I think it was in the fall of 2005), I was actually awakened by a loud crash, which sounded like the entire back of the house had collapsed. When I investigated, of course, I found nothing wrong. One of the most vivid of these experiences occurred at the end of my residency (during the fall of 2006). I was awakened from a deep sleep by someone coming up to the edge of my bed, and calling out my name. It was definitely a woman's voice that I heard.

Most of these ghostly experiences occurred during the night. As the reader might imagine, toward the end of my residency I was afraid to be in the house alone."

As a paranormal investigator, I can understand her feelings of fear and growing apprehension. Although not a single apparition was witnessed in the home, this doesn't lessen the experiences, nor the uncomfortable knowledge that she was sharing her house with an unseen resident.

Emma's Unseen Resident

When Emma moved into her new house, she never really believed that a house could be haunted. She'd heard of many tales through the years, but never had an actual experience. Certainly, when she was moving into this 100-year-old farmhouse in Elsie, future experiences with the paranormal were not on her mind. Emma did not know much about the history of this historic property other than the previous owner died at the age of forty-two, after a lengthy battle with cancer.

Emma's first experience with the unknown occurred while a roommate was moving in. While relaxing with a good book, Emma heard a sound emanating from the living room. Thinking that either one of the cats was messing around with some of her roommate's possessions or even a possible mouse infestation, she entered the living room. She saw that the noise was not caused by any of the cats or mice. The only thing she saw out of place was two CD cases that were pulled out of the stack and lying down. Thinking that gravity must have taken effect, Emma returned to her book and erased the incident from her thoughts, but not for long. Only a minute after sitting down, the noise repeated itself, only this time a little louder. Confused, Emma return back to the living room and quickly noticed that the two CDs were now standing upright and lined back up with the rest of the stack.

Emma's next experience started to confirm her suspicions that something unseen may be sharing her house. While downstairs, once again reading her book, she could hear the unmistakable sounds of the cat's jingle bells rolling across the hard floor above her. Her first thought was who in the world could be playing with those balls. She had purchased the toys for her cats, but soon learned that they held a hatred for the balls, and never played with them. Emma turned on the upstairs light and peaked over the landing. In the hallway, she expected to see one of her cats finally deciding the give the toy a try. She was surprised to see absolutely nothing in the hallway, not a ball, or a cat. Making her way back downstairs and returning to her book, she told herself that she must have imagined the sound. She repeated this to herself even after she noticed that all the cats were downstairs with her.

A few minutes later, back on the sofa reading, she once again heard the distinct sounds of the jingle bells moving across the hallway floor. Emma jumped up and immediately counted the cats; they were all there. So who was upstairs playing with the cat's toys?

These strange occurrences weighed on Emma's mind, but she never suspected that her roommate would also have such experiences.

Late one night, her roommate rushed downstairs and stated, "You're going to probably think I'm crazy, but could you come up here for a minute?" Hesitantly, Emma followed her roommate upstairs and into the hallway that separates the bathroom from Emma's bedroom. Seeing nothing unusual, she started to question the woman, when her roommate asked if she smelled anything odd. Sniffing the air, Emma could not detect anything strange, but now she was feeling nervous with the prospect that her roommate may have been smelling smoke. With her friend's urging, she continues to smell the air. Emma still cannot smell anything out of place.

When her persistent friend told her to "wait a few minutes," Emma was starting to think that maybe her roommate really was losing her mind. While reaching for the bathroom doorknob however, she was assaulted with the same event that her roommate was subjected to only minutes before.

"I got hit, like a furnace blast, with the strongest smell of men's cologne you can imagine. It was so strong, that it made me nauseous. Other than the previous owner, no men have lived in this house since I bought it. And it was very clearly men's cologne, not women's."

The forays with the supernatural did not stop there. The entity in the home was apparently very fond of the antique chandelier that hung in the living room.

"The chandelier in the living room, I swear, does this Medusa-like dance about twice a week at 3 am. It is only the one in the living room that does this and, for the longest time, I thought it was simply my eyes playing tricks on me. Then one night I happened to be watching *Ghost Hunters* on TV and they were interviewing a woman who lived in an old home that she believed was haunted. She described one of the antique chandeliers doing the exact same thing. I mean, it was eerie listening to her because she was describing exactly what I had been seeing here!"

While the roommate was in conversation with a coworker about ghosts one day, she began to explain some of the strange phenomena that were occurring in the house. When the coworker asked where the woman and Emma lived, the fellow worker became excited and said, "Oh my God! My ex-brother-in-law used to live there. That house is haunted. That's why he moved!" This coworker continued to testify about the Amityville-like stories involving the old house and all her brother-in-law's experiences while residing in the home.

After conveying her latest discovery of information to Emma, it was decided that they should attempt to document the constant phenomena. The roommate spent hours upstairs, where the majority of the activity occurred, and executed audio recordings in attempts to collect EVPs. Though most of the audio sessions were in vain, they did record a loud whisper, possibly saying the roommate's name.

Emma's numerous experiences with the paranormal world grew throughout the years of her residency in this old house. Moving shadows and lights turning on and off became common occurrences in the home.

On March 12, 2007, an event happened that finally made Emma a true believer of the supernatural.

"I have an electronic treadmill that I dragged in from the breezeway. Therefore, one day, I am in the living room eating lunch and this treadmill starts by itself, right in front of my eyes. I got up, walked over to it, looked under it, looked at the on/off switch and it's in the off position. But it's running all by itself, with no human feet on the rails. I unplugged it and it stopped.

"Later the same day," Emma continues, "I'm in the kitchen fixing dinner when, all of a sudden, I hear this buzzing noise. Immediately, I recognize the sound and break out in gooseflesh because I know that thing is unplugged. I turn the burner off on the stove and slowly make my way into the living room where the treadmill is. The very first thing I notice is that it is not plugged into the wall. The three-pronged plug and cord are in plain view, lying on the carpet. The on/off switch is on the off position, the lights on the control panel were lit, and the digital numbers were racking up—and the treadmill was turning like someone was walking on it! Just about the time I was getting ready to bolt through the front door, it stopped."

Trying to be sensible, Emma tried to rationalize this episode. The treadmill had been originally plugged into one of the brand new outlets that the licensed electrician replaced during the previous winter. She talked to a couple of electronics experts about the possibility of something internally shorting out and causing the treadmill to start to run on its own. No explanation could be concluded.

Emma's home began to quiet down after the treadmill incident, and things went back to normal. Well, if you say normal as having unseen resident turning on and off your television at random times, even while you are a holding the remote.

Normalcy diminished one late night in September 2007. While watching television at 2 am, Emma was startled to hear the sounds of someone walking around in a closed-off bedroom upstairs.

"The cat and I both followed the footsteps across the ceiling with our eyes as they made their way from one end of the room to the other. My first thought was that this was no cat. The floor up there creaks a little, even when I walk on it, but this sounded like a full-grown man!"

When she hit mute on the television remote, the footsteps ceased. Once again, after making sure all the cats were with her, Emma came to the conclusion that she had an intruder in her home. Grabbing a cordless phone from the next room and a large knife from the kitchen, she settled on the couch, poised to call 911 with the next noise she heard. One of her cats stood at the base of the stairs, staring up the stairs with its fur raised. This only added to Emma's fear, as her cat has never behaved in such a fashion.

She remained where she was until she fell asleep at five in the morning.

The next day, she inspected the room where her visitor was heard. Nothing was disturbed. All the windows were still locked and the doors closed. She knew then that her overnight human intruder was actually an intruder from the spirit world.

Emma will always wonder if her unseen resident could possibly be the former owner. Dying younger than expected, maybe his spirit is still not ready to leave the land of the living, even though his body already has.

The Giltner Murder

Was it insanity or jealousy? No one will truly know the nature of this crime, but an email from a former resident has declared that the house now holds something of the "paranormal nature."

On the evening of December 8, 1936, beautiful Elizabeth Giltner was sitting in her living room awaiting the arrival of her best friend, Hope Morgan. A sparkling December wedding was planned for Elizabeth and her beloved fiancée Captain D.S. Babcock, and Hope was to arrive to help with the wedding invitations. Dreaming of walking down the aisle, Elizabeth never imagined that she would never see her fiancée or family again.

Unbeknownst to anyone, when Hope arrived at the Giltner House, she was already concealing a gun that she took from her father's home. Whether Elizabeth and Hope got into an argument or Hope began to feel suffocated by listening to Elizabeth's obsessive chatter about her wedding ceremony, the actual "trigger" will never be known.

While in the midst of addressing wedding invitations, Hope extracted her father's gun from her pocket and fired five bullets into Elizabeth's chest and heart, killing her instantly. After fleeing the Giltner residence, Hope returned the gun to her father's safe and then drove to Battle Creek, onto Kalamazoo, up to Portland, and then back down to East Lansing, where she was finally arrested the next day at a friend's house. Instead of attending Elizabeth's bridal shower, Hope was giving her confession to the detectives, and demanding to see a psychiatrist.

What was her reason for the senseless murder of her best friend? According to the police report it was "An intense impulse to kill." This confession also ran in the *Associated Press* on December 9.

"I did it on impulse and I don't know why. For about a year, I have frequently had the impulse to kill. I put the gun in the pocket of my coat before going to Elizabeth's house yesterday. All of a sudden, I felt I wanted to kill and I emptied the gun. Then everything went blank."

It will never be known if she truly had a psychotic break and gave into her impulses or if she had the makings of a clever defense plot. On December 15, Hope Morgan, age twenty-five, scrawled small notes of remorse on a page ripped from a magazine, fabricated a rope out of silk pajamas and stockings, and hung herself from the water pipes in her jail cell. A psychiatrist hired to evaluate Hope asserted that she was planning suicide all along when she turned the pistol on her best friend.

Having to deal with the immense grief of losing his daughter in such a hideous fashion, Michigan State College (now MSU) Dean of Veterinary Science, Ward Giltner, moved out of the home.

John's family lived in the house for three years. John could remember many occasions when he would be upstairs alone in the house and would hear the sounds of footsteps on the main floor. The entity loved to make noises in the kitchen and open up every single cupboard door.

Once night, John fell asleep on the couch in the television room. He was awoken abruptly at 3 am by someone walking by the couch. He could still see the darkened figure when he reached for the light. However, when light illuminated the room, the figure was gone.

John became curious about the strange happenings in the house and decided to ask some questions. He discovered that his family was not the only one that had experienced a figure standing over them while they slept. In the past, owners of the house would rent out the basement area to traveling businessmen. One such man complained the next morning of being awakened by the figure of a woman standing at the foot of the bed.

Gayle, another previous resident of the house, also had a supernatural encounter with this female entity, only in a more gruesome manner. She told of a time when she was walking into the living room, and was confronted by a female lying on the floor, with a dark stain across her chest. Gayle had no idea who this woman was. Thinking that maybe a victim of a crime had just wandered into her home for help, Gayle went into the next room to call the police. Upon returning to the living room to render aid, she was shocked to see that the woman was gone. She frantically looked around the house and eventually outside for the injured woman. No luck. The woman had simply vanished.

Gayle explained that she never saw the female again, but after learning the history of the home, she is positive that she saw the apparition of Elizabeth Giltner, lying in a pool of blood in the exact place of her death. She declared that she felt sadness at times, with the image of Elizabeth's lost soul trapped in the house. Just as the residents before her testified, Gayle would also hear footsteps from someone unseen walking around the main floor of the house.

Is Elizabeth's tortured spirit still roaming the house trying to understand how the one person she trusted the most could have ended her life?

Katherine's Story

When Melinda's family moved into their new Lansing home, a haunted house was the last thing on their minds. Unfortunately, what they got was a grieving entity that made her presence known daily.

Melinda's mother was the first member of the family to come face-to-face with the supernatural. Deciding to stay home from work to continue with the chore of unpacking, she was home alone when she heard the definite sound of someone walking around in the attic area. Her first thought was a possible mouse infestation. Not particularly happy about that prospect, she ventured up to the attic to see how bad the infestation really was.

She was surprised by the lack of evidence of mice in the attic, but made a mental note to call an exterminator the following week.

As the days wore on, the knocking noises in the attic continued at all hours of the day and night. The exterminator found no evidence of mice and a plumber Melinda called in could not find any water pipes running through the attic floors that might explain away the knocking noises. Melinda decided that she would just have to accept the unusual banging noises coming from the attic and learn to ignore them.

One night, Melinda's daughter came into the bedroom complaining that the crying noises were keeping her awake. Confused, she asked her eight year old who was crying. The child did not know who was making the noise—just that she wanted it to stop. Now extremely curious, Melinda carried her daughter into the girl's bedroom only to be shocked by what she heard. Clearly, it was the sound of a woman crying. Melinda was not scared by what she was hearing; she was very disturbed by the lonely, heartbreaking tone of the woman's grief. She could tell that the sound was emanating from above her, from the attic. She also knew at that moment that she was dealing with something paranormal.

Melinda stated that she never felt threatened by the entity in the attic, as the spirit never seemed to leave the attic area to roam the rest of the house. The children adjusted to the unusual noises and quit asking for the sounds to go away.

During a quiet weekend away from the children, Melinda took this opportunity to spend the day in the attic and rummaged through some old trunks that had been left behind by previous owners. At the bottom of a large dusty trunk, Melinda's hands came in contact with what she felt was a large picture. Lifting up her newly acquired treasure, she came face-to-face with a portrait of a beautiful young woman in a flowing red gown. Melinda was not only struck by the beauty of this lady, but that her eyes seemed very haunted. She had to find out who this young lady was. Inspecting the back of the portrait, the name Katherine was written lightly on the back. Not knowing if this was the mystery woman's name or the painter's name, she decided to inspect the remaining trucks.

Her determination paid off. In a small leather box hidden in the back corner of another trunk, she discovered several letters dating back to the late 1800s. After reading several lines, Melinda realized that she was reading love letters between a fellow named James and a girl called Kate. Could this be the beautiful Katherine from the portrait?

The further Melinda delved into the letters, the tragedy of Katherine's life soon unfolded. Katherine was only nineteen years old and had fallen in love with a wealthy young man. The couple had a beautiful romance until the unthinkable happened—Katherine became pregnant. In the culture of the 1890s, unwed pregnant women were considered to be shamed souls, performing unspeakable sins. It was obvious from the letters that James felt that he had his whole life ahead of him and had no intention of marrying the frightened girl.

Katherine's story haunted Melinda for months. What became of this young woman and her unexpected child? She had to know more about the tragic love story.

Along with her sister, Melinda researched old records of Lansing's past citizens and of the house that she now resided in. Buried within the city's archives, Melinda discovered the result of Katherine's love affair. She came across a death certificate with the young girl's name and searched through the obituaries for that specific date. She soon learned that Katherine, frightened with the prospect of dealing with her pregnancy, decided that her life was over and death was her only answer.

Although no suicide note was ever found, it was labeled as a suicide by the local doctor. Katherine had hung herself with a rope from one of the attic rafters, near the doorway.

With the mystery solved, Melinda could never imagine what life had to have been like for Katherine and her grief-stricken decision to end her own life as well as the life of her unborn baby.

The banging and the pitiful crying continue to radiate from the attic to this day, but now Melinda understands the nature of the haunting in her home. She just prays that someday Katherine's tortured spirit will move on from this world and find peace at last in a better world.

The Dead Never Leave

Not many people would be able to live in a house that was once a funeral home. That is exactly what Sam does. In a large old Victorian home that had been converted into two separate apartments, Sam shared his lower-level apartment with two other friends. None of them knew the history of the house when they first moved in, but thanks to neighbors, they soon learned of the homes macabre past. Even more startling to one of the roommates, was the realization that his bedroom was once the "sitting room" utilized in long-ago funerals.

The first event that caused Sam to think that something was not "right" about their house was the strange electrical disturbances in the living room. One day, when it was time to leave, Sam turned off the television and placed the remote down on the couch. When he turned to walk out of the room, the television turned back on. Not giving it a second thought, he picked up the remote and turned the television off again. A few seconds past and the television turned back on again. Getting frustrated, Sam forged the remote and turned the television off by hand. This time the TV remained off. Sam made a quick mental note to replace the batteries in the remote and then left for the evening.

Sam returned home after midnight that same night. While walking through the living room to turn on the light, he was shocked when the television suddenly turned on with earsplitting volume. He immediately looked over towards the couch to scold one of his roommates for scaring him, and then he realized that he was alone in the room. He turned the television off, but the event unnerved him.

The next day went on uneventfully, until Sam went to bed that night. Still unsettled about the event that occurred the day before, he had trouble falling asleep. After midnight, he was awakened by the sound of music. Confused as to why one of these roommates would play the radio so late, he marched downstairs to confront his insensitive friend. He was startled to find that no one was in the room.

This time, one of his roommates also joined Sam in the living room, demanding to know why the radio was on. Sam replied that he was awakened by the same noise and had no idea who turned on the stereo. Upset, the roommate turned off the stereo and both friends started to leave the room. However, they only got a few feet when the radio turned back on again. Looking bewildered at each other, the roommate returned to the stereo and turned it back off. Standing there for a few moments, the radio remained silent. Satisfied that they could both return to bed, they were shocked to hear the stereo turn back on when they reached the next room. Now irritated, the roommate stomped over to the stereo and unplugged the system from the wall. Relieved that they could finally get some sleep, both men returned to their beds.

Sam was almost asleep when he heard the faint sounds of the radio once again. Lying there in the dark, he decided that he did not want to know if the stereo was still unplugged or not. He eventually heard the music turn off, but he never dared to venture in the living room.

This activity with the television and stereo continued for the next three days, always in the same room of the house. Then as quickly as it started, the unusual activity ceased. Things went back to normal for many months.

Normal was to eventually be broken when Sam and the roommates started to notice that items in the house began to disappear, sometimes for days at a time, and then reappear either where they were originally placed, or in completely absurd locations. One room-mate would constantly accuse Sam of stealing his library books. The books would disappear from his bedroom and eventually turn up a few days later, exactly where he'd left them.

This activity would also last for a few days and then end for several months at a time.

Within a couple of years, Sam would get used to the strange oc-currences and come to accept that he had to share his residence with the eternal guests from decades gone by.

The House of Evil

Rachael never lived in the house near Holy Cross Cemetery, but that does not stop her parents from talking about the frightening occurrences that now make them grateful that they no longer live in the home. In the 1960s, Rachael's family moved into the house on Saginaw Street a few short years before Rachael was born.

It was obvious from the beginning that there was something wrong in the house. Everyone was constantly engulfed with the feeling as if something unseen constantly watched them day and night.

This was confirmed with Rachael's mother a few weeks later. In her sewing room, she was interrupted once again by the feeling that someone had entered the room, but when she looked around, no one was there. She tried to shake off the oppressive feeling and return to her sewing. Within a few minutes, unable to ignore the intense feel-ing anymore, she looked over her shoulder only to discover that the attic door was now open. Feeling very hesitant, she slowly rose from her chair and walked towards the attic door. When she was a few feet away, the attic door suddenly slammed shut with immense force.

The family never felt comfortable in their home. They all believed that something very angry and sinister was living in the house with them. Everyone in the household would be awoken in the middle of the night by the sound of the basement door opening and slamming shut repeatedly. No one had the courage to go into the basement and lock the door. They also knew that the attempt would be in vain, as the angry entity would only find another door in the home to open and close all night. Terrified, all the family members refused to leave their beds, hoping that the activity would soon end.

When the family did venture into the basement during the day, they were assaulted by the lights going on and off and the feeling that the entity was standing directly beside them. Majority of the time, the family refused to enter the basement for any reason.

Many times, Rachael's mom would walk into the toddler's room after his afternoon naps to find the young child standing up in his crib, talking to someone unseen in the nearby rocking chair. The mother never liked the horrible vibration she would get from this event, as if something evil was in the room with her son. The son, when he was in his 20s, would describe to his mother that a lizard-like man would sit in the rocking chair in his room, asking him questions about the family.

To make matters worse than they already were, the family started to have strange misfortunes surround them. A fire of unexplained origins started in the parents' bedroom, the father suddenly lost his job, and the mother came down with a life-threatening illness that caused her to be hospitalized. Through all this, the family still continued with the daily struggles of lights going on and off, doors opening and slamming shut at all hours, and the constant feeling that they were never alone, never safe.

The family soon moved from the house. Rachael's family then learned that every family prior to their living in the home had lost a child to various tragic accidents, outside in front of the house. Rachael's family knew that they had just barely escaped that destiny, and equally sure that if they would have stayed, that destiny would have become reality. They felt especially fortunate. The sad thing was that they heard that the family that moved in after them also lost a child, victim of a traffic accident.

Haunted Childhood Memories

When I first learned of this house, I honestly believed that the sinister entity that stalks families from the Saginaw Street house followed the family to their new home. This is another story of Rachael's family, in their new home on Jerome Street. This is the home the family resided in when Rachael was born in 1965.

During an interview, Rachael discussed paranormal events that would happen on a daily basis. The activity experienced included lights turning on and off, items flying across the room, objects disappearing immediately after you set them down and then turning up several weeks later in odd locations around the house, and black shadows moving throughout the house.

There was one thing different with this house from the previous house. As Rachael stated, "We never felt uncomfortable in the house. We didn't feel evil. It was just there."

Rachael has an entire childhood full of memories of this house but a few specific episodes stick out in her mind above all else.

When Rachael was fourteen years of age, she was talking on the telephone and absently playing with an opal necklace that was hanging from her neck. After her hour-long conversation with a friend, she returned to the living room to watch television with her mother. She had just laid down on the couch and reached to play with her opal necklace when she realized that it was gone. Dismayed, Rachael asked her mother to look in the bedroom where Rachael was just talking on the phone. She was sure that the necklace must have slipped off her neck while she was fiddling with it and was now sitting on the bed or on the floor near the bed.

No sooner than Rachael made her request when something fell from the living room ceiling and fell on her chest. Rachael's mother flew up from the couch quickly and asked what that was.

Rachael placed her hand on her chest and found the necklace now sitting there. She held up the jewelry and said to her mother, "It's my necklace. I guess you don't have to look for it when you go to bed tonight." Rachael laughed when she talked about how her and her mother didn't watch television anymore that night; they sat on the couch staring up at the ceiling instead.

Another episode that Rachael clearly remembers occurred in the dining room. She had been doing homework and using a pen that was given to her as a special present from a friend. When she was finished, she noticed that the cap to the pen was missing. Unhappy, Rachael looked under the papers on the table and the whole floor underneath. She did not find the cap to her pen.

For the next two weeks, the hardwood floors were swept daily, but the cap never surfaced despite all the cleaning. Rachael, saddened that she had lost a part of her treasured pen, accepted the idea that the cap was gone forever—until one day when she was walking up the basement stairs and into the kitchen. An unusual sound occurred. Rachael was startled to see the cap of her pen rolling across the kitchen floor and stopping at her feet.

Tragedy soon erupted in the home when Rachael's mom passed away. Rachael recalls one episode that occurred approximately one week before her mom died. The paranormal activity increased at an alarming rate. Late one night, while sleeping in her bed, she was violently grabbed out of her bed and thrown across the room. At the same time, Rachael described that all her books and nick-knacks from the shelves were flying across the room as well.

"Often as someone is preparing to pass over, paranormal activity can become very active as the 'portal' to the other side begins to open," Rachael states. "I think that night the 'door' to the next dimension was opened full force and I got caught up in it."

The intensity of paranormal events continued to rise further.

Rachael testifies, "As the week progressed, more unusual things happened, including pieces of furniture being knocked over and items in the bathroom being tossed across the room. We always had paranormal activity in our house over the years, but the week leading up to my mother's passing was the most active we ever had in the house."

8
The Hotel Kern

Seven years after being nearby the world's worst mass murder of children at Bath, Michigan, and just four years from emerging from the economic troubles of the Great Depression, the city of Lansing dealt with another horrific tragedy. The Hotel Kern fire is recorded as one of the deadliest hotel fires in history. *The State Journal*, printed that day, labeled this disaster a "tragic holocaust." and "central Michigan's worst catastrophe since the Bath School Disaster."

On the evening of Monday, December 10, 1934, the Hotel Kern was a magnificent brick 211-room hotel filled with laughter and bright lights. Its guest registry included some of the most powerful government officials of the time. Nevertheless, on Tuesday, the impressive hotel became a ghastly sight. Flames had fully engulfed the hotel before the fire department could arrive. There was no hope of saving the Hotel Kern.

The record cold temperature that night of only -1 degree Fahrenheit made the fire even more devastating; crowds assembled in the streets near the ruins to watch the ice-coated firemen squatting in the street, spraying streams of water on the smoking remains. Rescue workers also battled the freezing temperatures, having to treat both hypothermia and fire-related injuries.

The scene was so troubling that one onlooker quoted in *The State Journal* said, "No war-torn village in France ever presented a more desolate appearance than what they were presently beholding."

The fire, started at 5:30 am, and was fanned by a brisk northwest wind, which allowed it to sweep quickly throughout the hotel. So quickly, in fact, that many guests and employees were trapped in their rooms and perished. With a guest list of 215 persons that night, officials originally believed that at least half of the people had perished. Many of the victims met their deaths jumping from the upper floors windows onto the ground below. Several bodies were believed to be to be in the Grand River, where a number of people were reported to have sought refuge from the flames in the icy waters.

The final death toll would reach thirty-two people. The Hotel Kern's manager, David Monroe, was among the dead, along with six state legislators and Senator John Leidlein. Three of the six legislators, Henry Howlett, John Goodwine, and Charles Parker all perished when they jumped from their third-story windows.

A message of sympathy from President Roosevelt was delivered on Tuesday afternoon by way of Governor William A. Comstock. His wired message read as follows:

"I am greatly shocked at the news. Please give my heartfelt sympathy to all injured and especially to the wives and children of those who lost their lives. I hope very much that the first reports were exaggerated."

The former Hotel Kern site is now a small park along the river's edge in the middle of a busy downtown area. A historical marker is all that stands to remind residents and visitors of what once stood on this land, and the tragedy that took place.

However, to some people, this site also represents paranormal activity. Motorists passing by have witnessed ghostly apparitions roaming this now-peaceful plot of land. One person sent us a message for our book series Web site telling of her own encounter near the river's edge of the park.

"I was visiting the old Kern Hotel site at night and decided to walk along the edge of the river. About twenty feet in front of me was the body of a man lying on the ground, parallel to the river. Even though I was very scared that I was about to find a dead body, perhaps one of the several homeless people that visit this park, I decided to walk towards it. When I was about six feet away, I called out to it, and I sat there and watched it slowly dissipate. After it was gone, I knew I had just seen a ghost."

Site of former Kern Hotel and river where many victims jumped to their deaths, 2007. *Courtesy of Brad Donaldson.*

Several emails we have received were statements from people who were guests of the Radisson Hotel across the street. The unlucky people who had stayed in the rooms facing the park have reported several sightings of apparitions moving around the former hotel site. One person who contacted us decided to leave the Radisson and venture into the park to check things out for himself.

"From my hotel room window, I could see a woman in a long dress walking aimlessly around the park across the street. She looked either lost or that she was looking around for something. It was starting to get dark so I decided to go to the park and see if the woman needed any help. Upon entering the park, I couldn't find the woman anywhere. Suddenly I hear this screaming coming from the river. It sounded like someone in serious trouble so I ran down to the waters edge. There was no one in the water and the park area was completely deserted, but yet I could hear the screams coming from the water. It lasted for about another minute and then there was silence. I felt very disturbed at what I heard and while walking back to my hotel, I saw a memorial marker. I stopped to read it and then I felt scared. I was visiting from Tennessee and I had no clue about the history of the park. When I read that people died in a hotel fire at this location, I felt even more frightened. When I got back to my hotel room, I immediately closed the curtains. I didn't want to see anything again."

Most people believe the ghosts that roam the former Hotel Kern site are most likely the poor souls who perished in the fire on that cold December day, however, other people have theorized that some of the paranormal activity in the park can be attributed to the 9-11 memorial in the same park. The memorial is a portion of the former World Trade Center. This twisted piece of metal was once a steel support beam in one of the Trade Center towers. This theory comes from the long-believed idea that any object can hold the energy of a spirit, whether it is a car, a bed, or even a ring. This is one of the beliefs on why most museums have ghostly activity.

Whether you believe that spirits of the doomed Hotel Kern roam this park, or the tortured souls of those lives cut short on September 11th, believers will never dispute that this quiet park is haunted.

9-11 Memorial at former Kern Hotel site, 2007. *Courtesy of Brad Donaldson.*

Religious Haunts

Billy "The Ghost"

R everend Baird never imagined how his life would change after arriving to his new church approximately twenty-five miles from Lansing. The reverend was anxious to meet his new congregation and to begin to minister to those who shared in his belief in the word of God. Soon, Reverend Baird was forced to face something he would never have expected, a visitor from the beyond.

Just over a month after his arrival, a middle-aged parishioner asked the reverend if he had seen the church ghost yet. Surprised and amused, he asked her for more information. The woman went on to explain that the church was the residence to a noisy ghost by the name of "Billy." For decades, many parishioners have heard banging sounds and footsteps throughout the church. Intrigued, Reverend Baird decided to keep an open mind.

In the next few weeks, five other church members approached him at different times to inquire about the resident ghost. By now, the reverend was beginning to give serious thought to the possibility there might indeed be a resident spirit. In addition, it was not long before he started to experience things for himself.

Often, when Reverend Baird was alone in the building, he would hear the sounds of someone moving around in the church. The phantom noises included the entry door banging shut, footsteps, and the eerie sounds of something moving furniture in the fellowship area. There were times when the sounds were so convincing that he would even go inspect the rooms for physical signs that something had moved, but nothing was ever disturbed upon inspection. As the unexplained occurrences increased, so did his belief that something unseen roamed within the church walls.

Ed, a church volunteer and parishioner, was very familiar with the haunting. On Saturday mornings, Ed would often be the first person at the church to get it ready to open to the public. While working these early morning hours in the church, he too would often hear the sounds that had been haunting the reverend. Ed was often so sure he heard the door open, he was certain another volunteer had arrived and would venture off to see who had shown up, only to find no one there.

When interviewed by an author and world-renowned ghost hunter Reverend Gerald S. Hunter, Ed stated, "I can't tell you how many times I have encountered our ghost."

Emily, the former youth director, also has tales to tell about the haunted church. One such story took place ten years earlier when Emily was volunteering as a chaperone for a teenage fundraiser. At one point, while she was crossing the fellowship area, she could hear a voice coming from the sanctuary. Frustrated that the children were trespassing in a restricted area, she entered the sanctuary to remove the offenders; she found the room to be unoccupied. Later that night, another chaperone reported that she had heard the same thing. Both chaperones decided not to discuss the occurrences with the youths, but neither ever returned for another overnight event in the church.

The church secretary tries her best to ignore the haunting sounds, especially the sounds of footsteps upstairs near the kitchen. She knows that when she arrives at the church in the morning hours, she is going to be greeted by the sounds of Billy roaming unseen down the halls and opening the doors on his way. She refuses to go into the church after dark, a practice she hopes will ensure she never comes face-to-face with the ghostly resident.

Legends of this church haunting go back for generations. Many of the parishioners who originally reported the strange activity are now deceased; the origins of the haunting were not lost with those souls however. It has long been known by the locals that during construction, one of the workmen, a carpenter named Billy, was hammering near the top of the bell tower when he slipped and fell to his death. Everyone who is familiar with the haunting assumes that the noisy spirit is none other than Billy.

Some repairmen have become irate by the antics of the church's permanent maintenance man, and Billy is often accused of moving their tools. There was once a time when a repairman "misplaced" his tools while working in the basement, and while he was searching for them, the light in the basement was turned off on him several times. The lights came back on and he continued his search, however, when the lights went out yet again, it was the last straw for this worker. He marched up the stairs to confront the joker, and found his tools laying on one of the steps. Now a little scared, the worker demanded that the reverend remain in the basement with him until the work was complete.

Although several current parishioners have seen Billy lurking in the building, they are reluctant to talk about it. However, one recent encounter with Billy has left two parishioners with a powerful and lasting memory.

The two women, also church volunteers, met at the church to wrap the Christmas gift donations. They arrived after dark, one of them with her three children in tow. When they turned on the light in the foyer, they witnessed an incredible flash of yellow light that streaked across the room; this light show, accompanied by a popping sound, quickly was identified as the result of having tripped the circuit breaker. The two women went down into the basement to reset the breaker while the three children continued up the stairs with their arms full of presents and wrapping paper.

The women had just arrived at the breaker box when screams pierced the night. The children, having only made it halfway up the stairs, came running down towards their mother. The two youngest children clung to their mother as if for dear life. They told the volunteers that there was a man standing at the top of the stairs. One of the children later described it further and claimed that the man was not standing but was actually floating above the floor, and after stopping at the stop of the stairs, he moved towards the kitchen, and then disappeared. When asked to describe the entity, they could only say he was a big man and that he was old.

The church haunting continues on to this day. Maybe one day, Reverend Baird will be able to come face-to-face with an unseen, devoted parishioner named Billy.

Can A Church Be Evil?

We know a church can house a haunting, but can a church be evil? For the purpose of this article, we will define church as the building and not the pastor or the congregation. Never in my life have I used the word evil to describe anything because it sounds so cliché and "Hollywood-ish," however, I cannot find a better way to describe the feelings my team retained from this old church.

My team, The West Michigan Ghost Hunters Society, came across an abandoned church during a paranormal investigation of the former Bath School Disaster site and every cemetery that was associated with it.

The investigation was going like any other until we reached Wilsey Cemetery, a site well known for the burials of Bath Disaster victims. What we were not expecting, is that the real activity would be in the desolate building that was directly across the street and that it would leave an impression that would forever haunt our memories.

The building was the former South Olive Methodist Church, built on Bond Road, about a half mile north of Round Lake Road. It was an old building as evidenced by the fact that its first meeting took place in 1885. From the beginning, the church seemed to suffer from bad luck, started with only ten charter members from a gift of $500 from Mrs. A. Wilsey. The church was constantly in debt and remained in debt until 1905, when congregation member Mrs. Door Wilhelm bequeathed at her death enough money to get the struggling church out of debt.

This shell, that once held lively sermons and the sounds of hymns, now stood as an unstable building, in an unkempt lot, directly across the street from the cemetery. Vandals had since broken some windows and the whole building looked like it was ready for the roof to cave in.

To us, this was an interesting, abandoned old church. Since Wilsey Cemetery was producing no evidence of paranormal activity, we decided to walk around the building across the road to have a look at it. Even before we crossed the property line, we all began to comment on the overwhelming feelings of oppression and negativity. In fact, at one point or another, every investigator present expressed feeling the "vibrations" of anger surrounding this building. Personally, this was a feeling that I seldom experienced, so as a result, I listened to my instincts and decided to remain at the front of the church even as most of my investigators ventured further onto the property to have a look around the back.

We were midway into our adventure when my father, WMGHS Investigator George Bray, started to walk up the front stairs to look inside the windows of this former place of worship. I decided to follow directly behind him. After only advancing up two or three steps, George stopped suddenly. This was the only time he would ever be witnessed hesitating on an investigation, and I snapped a picture to see if I could capture whatever it was that had scared this seasoned investigator on film. Moments later, he turned to me and said he refused to move any closer to this church.

What had stopped the man who had once investigated the haunted basement of a former morgue by himself with no fear or hesitation, and who had never displayed a second of fear during his many years with WMGHS? Whatever it was that stopped him, this man normally full of rock-hard bravery, now remained by the road rather than investigating the property.

By this time, most investigators claimed to have a bout with nausea whenever they got close to the church. This too was something that had been never before experienced during an investigation in the past. Due to this peculiar development, the heaviness in the air surrounding the building, and the ongoing feelings of something "evil" watching our every move, we decided to call it a night and leave this location. Nevertheless, this location will definitely never leave us.

On the trip home, I asked George about his experience and he stated that he felt this "great wall of anger" and all his muscles weakened, his heart started to race, and he felt like he was going to pass out. He stated that the feeling dissipated more with each step he took away from the church.

When I returned home that night, sleep was the farthest from my mind. I took this quiet time to glance over the photos I had taken from both the cemetery and the abandoned church. The photo that gained the most attention from me was the one taken from behind George, facing the front of the church. To the left of George was a distinct vaporous form near the front of the church. This photo represents to me the "presence" encountered by George when he attempted to go up to the front door.

A year later, I returned with another WMGHS investigator to this abandoned church. This time, the double doors that adorn the front of the former church, were standing wide open. As we approached the building, those same feelings of anger and heaviness returned. We forged ahead, but found it almost impossible to ignore the feelings of being "a prey in a hunter's paradise." When we approached the open front doors, we both took several pictures inside but neither of us ever went completely in. Standing in the doorway was enough, as it was incredibly hard to ignore the feelings that were emanating from this building. After hearing unexplained movement from inside the church, and having the feeling of nausea return, we decided that we could no longer remain.

When it was time to pull ourselves together and visit a third time, we found out through a volunteer from the Clinton County Historical Society, that the property was no longer a church, and in fact, a house now sits on the spot where the seemingly evil church once stood. It is a scary thought, thinking that whatever was on that property and in that church might now be haunting a family in the new house. Maybe that third visit might still be on our radar...

Investigator George Bray, moments before his chillng experience. *Courtesy of Nicole Bray, WMGHS.*

10
Olivet College

Michigan State University is not the only college in the Metro Lansing area that has a ghostly claim to fame. Olivet College also has its own resident ghosts.

The college was founded in 1844 by former slave owner turned abolitionist Congregational Christian, Reverend John J. Shipherd, and thirty-nine members of his congregation, collectively known as Olivetians after the first college they founded in Ohio, Oberlin College.

Ironically, paranormal activity in the form of divine intervention is often credited for the placement of the college where it is currently housed. When Reverend Shipherd set out to find land for his new college originally to be named New Oberlin, the original land for the college was to be in present-day Ingham County, approximately twenty-five miles from where the college stands.

Olivetian lore says that while Shipherd was on a trip to the site in Ingham County, his horse continued to get lost, and would always wander back to a hill above a swamp, which is where Olivet's Campus Square exists today. Shipherd believed that powers from above must have been drawing the horse back to this particular site, and deemed that "New Oberlin" should be located there. He instead chose to name it "Olivet," however, after the biblical Mount of Olives. Shortly after the founding of the college, Shipherd succumbed to malaria, as many other early Olivetians would.

The first classes of the newly-established liberal arts college were conducted in a log cabin. Today, Olivet College is a small campus consisting of many original buildings and a long history of paranormal activity.

Over the last century, there have been countless reports of paranormal activity, ranging from residual energy to poltergeist-type occurrences. Paranormal activity on the campus is not limited to the college buildings alone. Several students have reported seeing ghosts in a number of the historical homes that house students in the area.

Shipherd Hall

If there were a contest to be the most haunted building on campus, Shipherd Hall, obviously named after the college's founder, would be the front-runner of the paranormal games. In the case of this hall, poltergeist activity is the name of game with over 100 years of reports of objects being moved around in rooms, items materializing from nowhere, and even reports of items flying in and out of the walls.

Shipherd Hall, Olivet College, 2008.
Courtesy of Jeff Westover.

Stephen, a former Olivet student who resided in Shipherd Hall, will never forget one such incident. After returning to his room for his cell phone, he opened his door to find all of his textbooks neatly stacked in a tower fashion in the middle of the floor. A little surprised that his roommate would do such a thing, he left his room and decided that he would have a talk with his roommate when he got back.

Later on in the evening when Stephen returned from his study group, he discovered that the books were now stacked in rows on his bed. He was beginning to get frustrated with his roommates little antics, but his frustration turned into bewilderment, when he spotted a note from his roommate next to his computer, the note stated that he was taking a weekend trip with some other students. When questioned, Stephen stated that he clearly remembers that the door was locked each time he returned and that only two people had the key—his roommate and himself. So who had rearranged his books, not once, but twice; was it a ghost or a prankster? Stephen could not shake the eerie feeling that it was paranormal, but decided not to discuss the incident with his friend.

Another student, Daniel, explained that he became angry with his roommate for stealing a watch. His confused roommate denied knowing anything about his watch and was becoming very upset that Daniel felt that he could not be trusted. No more than ten minutes into the quarrel, the watch suddenly fell from the ceiling to the floor in between the students. That quickly ended the argument, but it did nothing to settle Daniel's nerves.

Daniel later discovered that others had experienced paranormal activity in this hall, when he discussed the occurrence with a female friend a few days later. His friend told him of a time when her boyfriend, also a Shipherd Hall resident, was sitting on his bed and was mesmerized when a glass of soda began to move back and forth across a table. The boyfriend was so terrified by the incident that he moved out of the Hall and into a nearby apartment with another student.

As if the students constantly being terrified by moving objects was not enough, unexplained music often plagues the security guards of Shipherd Hall. During semester breaks, the guards are responsible for touring the Halls to make sure that no break-ins have occurred. What they often find is faint music coming from an unknown location somewhere in the building. The guards have never been able to track the source of the phantom music, because it always stops before they can pinpoint its origin.

No area of Shipherd Hall seems to be immune to the unseen visitors. Many students have reported the sounds of footsteps in the basement. One student reported a time when he and some of his friends were in the basement area when they heard a child come running up behind them. Confused about what a child was doing in the basement, they turned around to see if they could help him. However, when they turned around, there was no one there.

Dole Hall

Dole Hall is also well known for its ghostly encounters. Built in 1931, this hall emanates the sensation of being watched by unseen eyes. One student claimed that no one ever feels safe while in the hall.

"Even when you are alone in your dorm, you're not alone. It's an intense feeling."

This same student also commented that the creepy feeling is worse in the basement, and many students have heard footsteps walking out of the laundry room, but no one would be there.

Dole Hall, Olivet College, 2008.
Courtesy of Jeff Westover.

Phantom music has often been heard coming from the Margaret Upton Conservatory of Music when no students are present. Once again, the security guards get the pleasure of hearing this supernatural orchestra. Upon investigation, no one else has ever been found to be in the building.

Alpha Lambda Epsilon House

Members of the Alpha Lambda Epsilon house are so used to their paranormal guests that they stated it as their "claim to fame" in the Olivet College 2004 to 2005 yearbook. They stated:

"Our house is haunted! People have been locked into rooms; at night, you can hear people walking up and down the stairs and loud knocks on doors, and some of us have actually seen things walking around. Derek Ott, one of our actives, actually saw a girl sitting in room seven. He described her as a faint glow, but with no eyes, just sockets. In addition, our house has two ghosts that have lived there since its opening in 1922. One is a little boy who likes to steal things from people. The other is an army veteran named "Red."

Alpha Lambda Epilson Greek House, Olivet College, 2008.
Courtesy of Jeff Westover.

The biggest speculation as to why this college could be haunted lies just to the south of the campus on Shipherd Street — Olivet Cemetery.

Olivet Cemetery

It is well documented that the original cemetery sat more to the north; in fact, it is known that several houses and Halls, such as Alpha Lambda Epsilon and Dole Hall, were built on top of the original graves. One document states, "When more buildings and housing were needed to expand with the growing student population, it was decided that the cemetery needed to be moved." Unlucky residents of this graveyard were then exhumed and relocated to the newer plots of land.

It is believed by many paranormal investigators that it was the moving of these bodies and the almost guaranteed fact that some bodies were missed, that has led to the activity in these buildings.

In the words of one elderly resident that lives near the college, "the spirits are just plain mad!"

Olivet Cemetery, 2008. *Courtesy of Jeff Westover.*

11
The Poor,
the Forgotten

Poor farm: Just the name conjures images of desolate and starving children, devoid of a happy childhood, working like slaves all day in the fields for nothing more than a little food, and a substandard education. This sad image is actually not far from the truth. Poor farms, in truth, were massive houses and farms that cared for the outcasts of society—people with mental and physical disabilities, the diseased poor, the elderly with no families, and young unmarried pregnant women rejected by their families. These people were often collectectively labeled by society as "paupers."

Historical marker, Ingham County Poor Farm Cemetery, 2008. *Courtesy of Joseph Stewart.*

On October 8, 1805, Michigan governors and judges created the "Act for the Relief of the Poor," the earliest law in regards to the relief of the paupers in the state of Michigan. These laws were modeled after similar laws in the state of New Jersey. With this first law, a pauper could petition three justices of the peace and had to prove that he or she was "destitute of support and was incapable of labor."

After a successful investigation by the judges, the paupers became "property of the public," and received state aid of no more than twenty-five cents per day.

In 1809, the law changed again, this time, mimicking laws of the state of Vermont. Michigan created a three-member tribunal, known as the "Overseers of the Poor." It would be these men who would now determine who was eligible for public support.

In 1817, more changes to the "Act for the Relief of the Poor" were adopted, this time borrowing from the neighboring state of Ohio. These changes created apprenticeships that the children of the destitute were forced to fill; this helped to create the sad image of children working in the fields and mills.

Over the next decade, many revisions to the laws passed, but it was not until 1830 that the Legislative Council passed an act authorizing the county supervisors to establish poorhouses. The first poorhouse in the state was established in Wayne County originally named the Wayne County Poorhouse; it is best known by its nickname Eloise.

Public Act 148 of 1869 revised and consolidated all previous acts relating to the support and maintenance of the poor. The law directed the county board of supervisors to erect more poorhouses, and required the education of pauper children between the ages of five and eighteen. These numerous poorhouses existed to house those who had "poor health, disease, mental illness, or other problems and no other means of support."

In 1909, poorhouses or poor farms received a more respectable name, county infirmaries. Eventually, all but one of Michigan's eighty-three counties had established a poorhouse. In 1938, there were still seventy-nine county infirmaries remaining, some with operational farms giving the origin of the term "poor farms."

Poor farm cemeteries are a depressing reminder of the forgotten. Adults and children who were residents of these institutions would often die of illnesses and injuries; the same illnesses that wealthy Michigan citizens would often recover from, given the proper medicine and care. Paupers, devoid of any money for a proper funeral, received the substandard burials, used by the state. Most of the deceased ended up placed either into small mass graves, or in a private unmarked pauper's grave. Some souls were lucky enough to have family members claim their bodies and received a proper burial elsewhere, or at the least have a family member pay for a gravestone.

Gravestone, Ingham County Poor Farm Cemetery, 2008.
Courtesy of Joseph Stewart.

These county cemeteries not only held the destitute who worked the farms during life, but also included other unfortunate souls, such as the homeless, unidentified bodies from murders and suicides, and prisoners. Burials in the Ingham County Home Cemetery range from the years 1890 to 1943.

The original graves were unmarked and randomly placed in the cemetery. Many of the grave markers are missing vital information on the deceased, such as first or last names, and some hold only a date of death or death age due to the lack of documentation on the citizens that society wanted to forget about. To make matters worse, sometime during the 1930s, the hired tombstone maker was obviously dyslexic as some stones have backwards letters and numbers.

Students from nearby Kinawa Middle School visited and researched the cemetery for their "Explore the Past" project. They were quick to note that there was a lack of gravestones from the 1920s. With the help of a local historian, it was discovered that during the 1920s, the Poor Farm received payments from a university for bodies obtained for research.

Ingham County Poor Farm Cemetery, 2008.
Courtesy of Joseph Stewart.

Therefore, there should be little wonder why these area cemeteries, filled with so much disease, pain, and trauma, can sometimes hold high amounts of paranormal activity. The first county poorhouse, Eloise (that later became an asylum), is notorious for its haunting experiences, has already confirmed this theory with paranormal enthusiasts. Based on the e-mails received by the authors from several individuals, it is clear that experiences with the supernatural are common in this local poor farm cemetery as well.

The first email received was from a woman named Anne, doing family genealogy research in the cemetery on a late June afternoon. Anne was perusing gravestones on the right side of the cemetery when an intense feeling overcame her.

"I felt goose bumps on the back of my neck and arms. I just knew I was being watched but I was sure that no one else was in the cemetery at that point. I didn't really like the feeling."

Anne tried to ignore the uneasy feeling and continue with her mission of finding her ancestor's grave marker. Nevertheless, after a while, the feeling was becoming too intense and she decided to leave and continue her search on a later day. She walked about thirty feet when she saw a figure off to the left. What caught her attention was that the male figure, approximately middle-aged, was wearing very old clothing and holding his hat in his hands. Anne, now familiar with period clothing after spending over a year looking at historical photographs, made the educated guess that the clothing was from the 1930s. This male figure simply stood there, looking down at the ground for several seconds, and then vanished before her eyes. Anne left the cemetery in a rush and later hired a researcher to continue her search. Anne states that when she mentioned her encounter at the poor farm cemetery, the historian simply said, "It happens a lot, ma'am."

"I have never seen anything like this before! I didn't believe in ghosts. Well, didn't believe until then," Anne now testified.

A sad-looking male apparition is not the only ghostly encounter that visitors have experienced in this cemetery of rejected souls. A group of local kids, who wanted to remain anonymous for obvious reasons, stated that they entered the cemetery at night to do some amateur ghost hunting. Armed with only one digital camera and a lot of courage, this team of rag tag thrill seekers stalked their way through the cemetery area, hoping to get the perfect image of a ghost captured on film. What they encountered was something auditory instead. The group, roaming their way through the illegible gravestones, was startled to hear the sound of children. The group, frozen in place, knew that small children would not be present in the cemetery this late at night; they also knew it was too late for the sounds to be coming from a nearby house. They continued to listen to these disembodied voices until they suddenly ceased as quickly as they began. The group said they did not waste any time leaving the cemetery grounds. They testified in their email that they were not sure if they would return to the location any time soon.

On our request, Joe and Kim from the Ghost Research Centre visited the location to partake in a photography project. Unbeknownst to us, they were also intending to perform audio recordings, in an attempt to capture EVP (electronic voice phenomena). Walking around the desolate graveyard, they spoke constantly to unseen entities in hopes of getting a verbal response. According to Joe, the ghost hunting pair definitely received responses.

At one point, Joe asked aloud, "What is your name?" The response was an eerie declaration from a male spirit that he did not remember what his name was, but spirit did leave a clue of his identity a few minutes later. Joe captured on digital the same entity stating a possible home city—San Diego.

Other EVPs include two female voices, and one of a male entity recorded in reverse. All EVPs captured during this excursion will eventually be posted on their team's Web site.

As a side note, I remember the first EVP that my team captured. It was also in a poor farm cemetery here in West Michigan. I had asked if anyone was there, and my response was a male entity whispering to me, but not clearly enough to make out certain words.

There are paranormal investigators who claim that cemeteries should have no more occurrences of hauntings than any other flat plot of ground; and that it is rather a matter of the entitys' attraction to the emotional energy of the living. Therefore, when the living leave the area, the paranormal activity should consequentially cease; however, with this theory it would seem any place an investigator focuses on would be active. So what is it about these cemeteries that seems to make them hold a higher level of paranormal activity? Do these forgotten souls defy paranormal reasoning and haunt the very areas where they were meant to rest in eternal peace? Could it be in the case of the paupers spirits, they have attached themselves to the graveyards, which in many cases, are the only evidence they ever even existed?

12
Strange
Dansville

Nestled in the heartland of Michigan, and just south of Lansing,
rests a small town that loves its local folklore and oddities.
The area, now the village of Dansville, was originally settled
in 1844 by Samuel Crossman
from New York. Daniel Crossman, Samuel's son, officially
platted the village in 1857,
naming it after himself and
the village's first postmaster,
Dr. Daniel Weston. Dansville
was not actually incorporated
as a village until 1867.

This small town, with a
population of less than 500,
has been described by visitors as a "creepy little town,
full of haunted allure."

Dansville Village marker, 2008.
Courtesy of Colleen Shunk.

Dansville Middle School

In the past, the Dansville Middle school used to hold all levels of education—elementary, middle, and the high school. With the growth of Dansville and its surrounding areas, the building is now used solely as a Middle School.

The beautiful bell tower that adorns the front of this building seems to be the center of one of the three paranormal "host spots" of this school. Local folklore has listed several different people as the tragic victim who fell from the bell tower. Research found references to a young girl that jumped from the tower; the story then changes so that the doomed teenager is a boy, and yet another tells of a disgruntle faculty member walking through the now-blocked door in the 8th grade math teacher's room, and jumping to his death from the same tower. The faculty member's version gets more complex with the legend that the spirit of the worker come back at the anniversary of his death and he can be seen walking to the tower and jumping off, forcing any unlucky individual to witness the residual remake of his suicide.

Whichever story you choose to believe, everyone agrees that the bell tower gives off an ominous feeling and makes people uncomfortable.

The third floor seems to hold more than just that fated doorway to the bell tower, and this repeating incident seems to be a little more on the credible side. If you are on the third floor when it's dark, which is easier in the early darkness hours of the wintertime, numerous students and faculty have reported an overwhelming feeling that could only be described by one person as "something heavy is clinging to your back" or a "gravity increase."

As if that feeling is not disturbing enough, some people have also claimed to hear whispered voices coming from the end of the hall and the eerie creaking sounds emanating from the stall doors of the boy's bathroom that is situated between the second and third floor landing. Others yet have mentioned the appearance of apparitions in the second-floor bathrooms. The sounds of footsteps and jingling of door handles are a commonplace during the dark and empty hours. One night janitor took to wearing headphones while he worked to block out the sounds of the frightening noises that he continuously heard.

This school holds yet another paranormal specter and this one can be found in the Auditorium. Despite technician inspections and brand new wiring installed, actors rehearsing their lines are interrupted by the lights on the stage and the balcony turning themselves on and off. Even more disconcerting is a dark figure that

Dansville Middle School, 2008. *Courtesy of Colleen Shunk.*

has been spotted repeatedly standing in the second-floor balcony, and clapping its approval at the end of every performance. One of the speculations about the entity is a reference found on a message board of a young person taking a "swan dive" off the balcony during a basketball game.

Faculty, students, and lighting technicians cannot confirm the theory of this dark figure that presides over plays and choirs, but all agree on the uneasy feelings surrounding the balcony area.

An online search for any other ghostly experiences at this institution only resulted in one other mention. This user-submitted Web site simply declared:

"The spirit of a female with half her head gone came into view in a Dansville secondary school at night wandering the halls. Numerous accounts of this ghost have been conveyed."

Could this statement be referring to yet another entity roaming the halls of Dansville Middle School?

The Octagon House

Built in 1863 during the throes of the Civil War, this architectural beauty is among one of the most recognizable structures of Dansville. Listed as one of Danville's oldest buildings, a photo of the house in 1978 clearly shows that renovations have taken place in recent years to preserve this historic home. Despite the fact that it is shaped liked an octagon, locals are more familiar using the name "Hexagon House."

Rumors of this house being used in the Underground Railroad have fueled the fire for this location to be nicknamed "the most haunted house in Dansville."

As most people know, The Underground Railroad was neither a railroad nor underground. Instead, it was a secret group of anti-slavery supporters who housed, fed, and guided slaves from different regions of the South and into Canada. Because Canada, a country that did not allow slavery, was very close to Michigan, citizens of Michigan played an important role in making the Underground Railroad successful. Because of the fame of this secret organization, no one was identified by their names. Instead, supporters who helped the slaves escape took to being called by railroad titles such as a conductor, a station manager, and a station agent.

Octagon "Hexagon" House, Dansville, 2008. *Courtesy of Colleen Shunk.*

There were at least seven known ways for the slaves to travel through Michigan and arrive in Canada. Two of the seven routes went through the Lansing area. The most well known route was the Grand River Trail running from Indiana and Illinois, to Benton Harbor, then to South Haven, into Holland, further into Grand Rapids, over to Lowell, onto Portland, into Lansing, onwards to Williamston, then to Howell, into Brighton, to Farmington, and ending in Detroit. From there, they were secretly transported across and into Canada.

Local tales that the Octagon House, with its secret doors and tunnel system rumored to run all the way to Lansing, have emerged and grown through the generations. The tales of Dansville's presence with the Underground Railroad does hold some merit. The North Branch School (built in the 1850s) was nicknamed "Little Africa" because of its secret room under the school floor that was utilized as a hiding place for slaves. This confirmed historical stop on the notorious Underground Railroad resides only fourteen miles north of the Octagon House in Williamston.

During an interview with an owner of a haunted home, the woman stated that her grandmother used to live in the odd octagon-shaped house and confirmed that there are indeed tunnels under the structure. "Lori" remembers her grandmother showing her the doors to the tunnels and telling her what the tunnels were used for in the past.

Many locals of Dansville testify that the house is haunted by former slaves who exploited the property for safe passage to a new and free life. Visitors to the house claim to hear banging and knocking noises coming from the tunnels, despite that some areas of the tunnel are currently collapsed and have not been used for over a hundred years.

Locals have declared looking into the windows at night and seeing faces and strange lights bouncing in the rooms. Are these spirits of beaten and bruised slaves, full of terror at the possibility of being captured and returned to cruel masters, still hiding in the dark tunnels and basements?

The Haunting
Of Seven Gables Road

One of the most well know legends resides approximately two and one half miles southeast east of Dansville, and rests in the Dansville State Game Area.

When you talk to the local citizens, there appears to be two different legends for the same area, but somewhat tied into one another. This is also one of the most confusing legends I have ever read because of the different variations. This may be written off as a local urban legend, but people who have visited this area believe that something unseen is stalking the land.

At the end of Seven Gables Road, there is a gate in front of a path that leads far into the State Reserve land. Young people galore flock to this area to see if the tales of paranormal activity and the legends are true.

The first legend states that a house used to be located just past the gate. One night, an unknown assailant broke into the home, terrorized a family of six, and then one by one, hung them from the rafters.

Dansville State Game Area; Seven Gables Road, 2008.
Courtesy of Colleen Shunk.

After finishing his insane deed, he set fire to the home to cover any evidence. Another version of the same story is that the killer committed suicide on the property after setting the house on fire.

The second local legend refers to a practicing witch who formerly lived on property that is now a part of the Dansville State Game Area. She was a bitter and hateful woman who had placed a curse on the land. This curse was to include the death of anyone who dares to enter the property. According to local folklore, if anyone trespasses onto her property and hears the sound of the witch screaming, the last person to make it over the gate is cursed to die. Some locals have told the tale of how there were seven children who came upon the witches house and she killed them. On this same property, twenty-five years later, the first legend supposedly occurs. Dansville locals claim that it was the witch's curse that caused the father of a family of four to go insane, burning down his house with the family inside, and then hanging himself from a tree on the property.

All legends aside, this State Game land has seen real tragedy and death. During an interview for another chapter of this book, the gentleman being interviewed mentioned a documentary from a local cable network that aired a story about the State Game area. They mentioned a possible drowning in one of the lakes and the journalists also stated that they stumbled upon a small cemetery. Research that I have done surfaced no such cemetery, but the gentleman stated that this documentary showed the journalists pushing overgrown brush away to reveal small headstones.

This possibly cursed area is also infamous as the perfect location for dumping bodies. No one will be able to forget the recent heartbreaking story of little Ricky Holland, whose body was disposed of in a marshy area of the State Preserve. Just as poignant, but long forgotten, is the murder of Laurie Murninghan, former Lansing Mayor Max Murninghan's daughter. On July 9, 1970, Laurie was kidnapped, raped, and strangled with her body being dumped in the State Game area, twenty feet into the woods at Barnes and Meridian Roads. Three boys searching for pop bottles found her.

Through an internet search of Seven Gables Road legend, I found several people who openly talked about their experiences at Seven Gables Road.

One woman and her husband decided to take a daytime hike on the trail. After they passed the lake, they came across the remnants of an old cobblestone road. It was then that they noticed the eerie silence, no birds, no animals, not even the breeze blowing; a strange unexplained stillness. Upon looking at their surroundings, they spotted what appeared to be four or five piles of wood. Figuring that this could be the legendary former home of the witch, they turned around to return back to their vehicle. That is when their simple exploration trip for the ruins started to turn into a trip in the supernatural. During their journey, they started to notice things that were not present when they first walked the trail. The first thing the couple noticed were odd shaped items hanging off the tress. The wife could only explain the shapes as appearing like "colored paper in weird shapes." The sudden smell of sulfur permeated the air, and with the combination of the ensuing darkness that was approaching, they quickened their steps. After several feet, the husband stopped his wife in her tracks and pointed up the path. There, snagged on a log, was a piece of material that was not present during their initial pass down the trail. The wife could only describe this cloth as "an old kind of material that was stained and ripped. The couple decided to take the item with them. By this time, the sky was getting extremely dark and the odd sound of someone unseen following beside them in the field could be heard. The air seemed to be getting thicker and it was getting harder to breathe. Within sight of their car, panic began to set in as the couple felt that the path was closing in on them. The wife screamed to her spouse to discard the material items that they took. Thunder and lightning suddenly overtook the blackened sky as the couple raced for their vehicle. Just as they got inside their car, they were bombarded with hail. Upon driving up the road to the stop sign, the wife looked back to discover that the sudden furious storm was only over the State reserve land, and nowhere else.

Later in bed, the woman was resting and thinking back on her adventure on Seven Gables Road when there was unexplained tapping on her forehead. For that night, and up to three nights afterward, there was a series of strange phenomena in her home, including a picture of her son that would fly across the room and hit the far wall.

Despite this disturbing experience in the unknown, the wife returned to the trail, but this time it was late at night and other friends were present. Upon walking down the path in the darkness, they group was surrounded by a sudden wind and a deep feeling of nausea. No word if this was the wife's last foray with this popular haunted location.

Other reports from souls courageous enough to venture into these darkened woods, not to mention an eerie section of the trail that has been described as "the black hole," have talked about hearing the sounds of children playing in the woods, the ominous banging noises of metal hitting on wood, and something sinister following you down the trail. After listening to the tales about this cursed and scary place, we had to visit there ourselves.

Our first visit to Seven Gables Road occurred on a warm September day. When arriving at the end of this doomed road, we were met by an SUV full of young people who also heard about the legend and had ventured out to see the area. After steadfastly refusing to go past the gate and down the trail, the visitors left. We decided to go past the fence and see the area for ourselves. About 300 feet down the trail, I met up with a local woman who was walking her dog. I stopped and asked her about the local ghost legend. She did not deny anything of the legend, but simply stated that the foundation of the house is not on this part of the State Reserve land, but east of Seven Gables Road. Due to the lateness of the day, I made a mental note to have this information checked out for our next visit to the area.

A worker from the nearby farm, "Rod" stopped us on the trail to discuss the Seven Gables Legend. Many local farmhands believe that a witch placed a curse on this land to make the land uninhabitable.

After some minor research online, and tagged with immense help from Colleen Shunk, the founder of the paranormal team Mid-Michigan Ghost Hunters, a few more facts were soon discovered about this local tale. Colleen knew of a local woman who currently lives on Seven Gables Road. After a quick call to this woman, information was revealed that Dansville State Game Area held many foundations from previous homes. The state of Michigan forced many homeowners to leave the area due to rattlesnake infestation. Okay, not as dramatic as a witch and a mass murderer stalking the land, but snakes can give anyone the creeps. But I was also struck by the statement that Rod had mentioned earlier. A rattlesnake infestation sure would make the area unfit for humans. to live on.

With plausible story of snakes in the back of my mind, and since our first visit to this haunted land deemed a little disappointing, I decided to post to a message board that I was looking for experiences at this location. I was not prepared for the responses that I would soon receive.

The first report was from a group of friends who decided to check the place out for themselves. Ignoring the leaf crunching noises that were following them on the right, they could not ignore the green smoky-looking figure that crossed the path a few hundred feet in front of them. After being paralyzed by fear for several minutes, the group gathered their courage to continue their journey. About a quarter of a mile down the path, they described the trail as suddenly "turning pitch black and all the normal noises made by bugs seemed to stop." The eerie feeling continued to grow stronger, so the group decided to leave.

A father and son drove to the Seven Gables Road area after the father expressed curiosity about the legends that he had heard. His son had been to the frightening location once before. Arriving at the turn-around area and driving towards the gate, the father declared that both him and his son unexpectedly felt "cold chills pass through them." The son abruptly turned to his father and vowed, "There are not very nice spirits here and we gotta go now." Upon heeding his son's strange declaration, the father drove away from the gate. Approaching the hill, the father looked in the rear view mirror only to witness a faint orange-green light hovering over the trail past the gate.

Another large group of teenagers decided to challenge the "witch." Walking down the path, two boys simultaneously spotted a white figure coming up the path towards them. One of the teenagers, arriving at the foreboding location armed with a camera, took a picture down the path. Once they arrived safely at their car, they looked at the photograph and were surprised to see six bright balls of light where the "apparition" was witnessed only seconds before.

There are numerous other stories that have emanated from this one, but the majority of them all talk of a heavy, eerie feeling that surrounds visitors, witnessing misty apparitions, and the foreboding sounds of screaming.

With all these tales circulating about this one location, I decided that it was worth a second trip and a further look into the area behind the legend.

Arriving at the location, this time at night, I was hoping to witness some of the phenomena that everyone else was whispering about. Armed with a digital camera, IR infrared thermometer, and Tri-Field EMF detectors, we ventured past the cursed gate and down the path. I was to come away extremely disappointed in the lack of "supernatural drama" during our foray. There were no documentable temperature variances or EMF spikes. A misty apparition did not appear to us; the only thing that was noticed was the amount of coyote activity in the area. When the coyotes cried out, it sure sounded like bizarre screaming. I was left wondering if we just debunked part of the legend, the part where you hear the witch or the suffering children screaming in the night! We called it a night and decided to come back the next day to investigate the area more in the daylight.

Upon our return the next morning, we found something very interesting that may add to the supernatural activity that people claim to encounter on this State land. Forget about old witch curses; we found evidence of modern witchcraft! Walking along the trail, I spotted something round that was bright orange. Expecting to find an old

Trail through Dansville State Game Area; site of paranormal activity, 2008. *Courtesy of Brad Donaldson.*

child's ball, I pushed the brush back to discover it was an orange, and near it were a couple of apples. Finding it odd to find several pieces of fresh fruit in the middle of the woods, I investigated the immediate area. I found burned candles. When I asked Rob, a Pagan High Priest about my find, I was told that it appeared to be the Wiccan ritual for the dead. The fruits are a symbol of sacrifice to Mother Earth. Was this really just a ritual to bring peace to the tormented souls that roam this place, or was there a darker agenda behind this ritual?

Needless to say this got my mind reeling. There are a plethora of documented cases where a location did not possess paranormal activity until unskilled amateurs had attempted pagan or satanic rituals, much the same as playing with an Ouija board, to make contact with the dead. To learn more about this, visit the chapter, "Theories Behind a Haunting."

With this new discovery, I was left with the obvious question of whether Seven Gables was haunted by entities and curses from the past, or the continuous results of modern-day conjuring of something sinister that now plagues the land.

Regardless, this legend intends to live on for generations to come.

The "Burning Bed"

I vaguely remember this 1982 movie from my childhood. The scene I can recall the most was Farrah Fawcett setting a house on fire, with her husband in it, and driving away while her kids, also in the car, were screaming at her and watching the flames as they all drove away. What I did not know at the time was that this movie was based on a true story, and the real-life location of the death of an abusive husband in the small town of Dansville, Michigan.

Francine Hughes, a Michigan housewife, had endured over thirteen years of extreme physical and emotional abuse, plus isolation and futile attempts for help from local officials. To end her years of suffering, Francine made a fateful decision on the night of March 9, 1977. While her husband was sleeping in a drunken stupor, she poured gasoline all around the bed, lit the match, and burned him alive. Francine was evidently charged with first-degree murder. The case did go to trial, and Francine was found "not guilty by reason of temporary insanity."

Little is now known about Francine Hughes, but I did find a couple of references of drug addiction in an attempt to sedate her painful past, and references to the fact she remarried, but sadly to another abusive male.

There is a new house in the place of the former burned-out structure, but for the privacy of the current resident, I will not disclose any pictures that I have obtained of the current home or the true address of the property.

Locals have testified that you can hear the sounds of a man screaming in pain if you get close to the house in the darkness of night. Could the tortured soul of this husband be forced to relive his painful demise for eternity?

13

Ghosts of Medicinal Means

The Children of the Clinic

f you drive around the city of Lansing, Michigan, you will see some of the most beautiful displays of architecture ever created in the state. The vision of Michigan's Capitol building alone is breathtaking. However, in some of the oldest neighborhoods in Lansing, it is not just the architecture that can attract attention, but also the unseen residents that lurk inside the buildings.

We investigated one such house in Lansing, built over 127 years ago. Its beautiful structure stands out today amongst the concrete streets and bustling traffic. What was previously a house is currently a medical office that holds not only patients and staff, but also invisible denizens that make their presence known from time to time.

One visitor to the medical clinic, who was sensitive to the spiritual world, immediately sensed entities when she entered the office. Within a few minutes, she noticed the vibrations of two children still residing in the building. One child, described as a young boy smitten with the medical receptionist, would often peek at her from around the corner in the hallway. The presence of the entity could explain the sometimes-extreme cold spots often felt in the reception area.

The other child was a little girl that liked to sit on the boxes stacked in the physician's office and took joy in watching the doctor at work.

This statement" was a little disturbing to the doctor since the visitor who was still standing in the reception area, had never visited the clinic and had no physical way to know that the doctor had recently stacked boxes near his desk in his office.

The children, when not watching the medical staff, often would hide out in one of the storage rooms. This revelation explained a great deal as the doctor and his receptionist had often heard scratching and knocking noises coming from the small storage room. The sound of children giggling is a disconcerting experience that happens in the building on an almost weekly basis. The doctor reported that he would often find the storage door open and the light on when he returned to his clinic in the morning after being locked up for the night.

On one occasion, the physician decided to surprise the children by opening the door in a sudden motion, and was stunned to hear the sound of a gasp and the noise of small feet shuffling to the back of the room. To this day, the doctor will knock before entering the storage room and the receptionist refuses to go into the room altogether.

The doctor has reported the unexplained yet familiar odor of pus and infection from time to time in the hallway leading to the storage rooms.

The sensitive also picked up on the vibrations of a couple living on the upper floor. Once again, the doctor became very amused because there was no way the visitor could possibly know of the activity heard constantly from the second floor.

According to the staff, the second floor is a Mecca of paranormal activity such as the sound of footsteps walking the darkened halls and doors slamming at an alarming decibel. Often the doctor would investigate the strange noises only to find that he was alone in the building and all the doors on the upper floor were still locked. Perhaps this is the couple's way of validating their continued existence in the building.

One experience that the doctor says he will never forget is the time he witnessed a gray figure, devoid of any details or a face, walk from the hallway near his office and into the reception area.

These experiences prompted the scientific-minded physician to contact someone who might be able either to explain away all the strange occurrences in the building, or to gather scientific evidence to lead to a conclusion that the building may be authentically haunted.

Five days before Halloween, the West Michigan Ghost Hunters Society accepted the doctor's request to investigate the building for paranormal activity and journeyed to Lansing. Three investigators, founder Nicole Bray, EVP Specialist Robert DuShane, and geologist Bob Webster participated in the investigation.

After touring the building and hearing the stories of paranormal activity, the team went to work setting up four cameras and creating an agenda of locations for audio recordings. One camera was placed in the storage area, with a toy placed in the room as a "trigger item" for the children to play with. Camera number two was situated in the reception area, facing the stairway and the hallway leading to the doctor's office and exam room. Camera number three was placed in the hallway on the second floor in hopes of capturing the residual activity of footsteps and doors slamming. Base temperature readings remained steady at seventy-four degrees Fahrenheit. A general sweep to check for high, and sometimes dangerous, EMF levels came back with nothing that needed immediate concern; this further validated the need for investigation since high levels, sometimes caused by very old electrical wiring in a building, have been associated with paranoia and hallucinations.

Four minutes after midnight, while all three investigators were monitoring the cameras, each camera, one by one, went offline, but did not lose power. It is not uncommon to lose one camera due to an electrical disturbance or interference, but this is the only time we have ever lost them all. This event lasted approximately five seconds and then all cameras came back on at the same time. No explanation was ever found for the cameras' weird malfunction. Following protocol, investigator Robert DuShane suggested an immediate audio session in case the entity remained on the second floor, near the equipment.

Halfway through the audio session, the smell of roses permeated the air around the two male investigators.

Later on in the night, investigators Rob and Bob went into the storage room for another audio session. The purpose of the session was an attempt to make contact with and record the voices of one or both of the children. Midway into this experiment, Rob felt something hit his arm. We later checked the video camera that was running in the storage room through the entire investigation, and confirmed that Rob did not bump into anything in the room, but his reaction to being touched was obviously genuine.

We expected more evidence to be revealed when we analyzed the data, but other than the spooky things we experienced at the site, we had just a possible EVP to add to the mix--though there were too many other human voices interfering to make it a sure thing. Even the doctor was hoping for the children to play with the toy in the storage room. Still, questions remain: What happened to the cameras? Whose perfume were we experiencing? And who touched Rob? We know that both the investigators and the medical staff have had a lifetime's worth of memories of ghostly penenomena surrounding them as they worked with their patients...and maybe more to come.

Sparrow Hospital

Hospitals are notorious for their haunting experiences and ghostly apparitions. Where else, besides battlefields, would there is such a high level of pain and death? With everyday occurrences of deaths in the Emergency Rooms and Intensive Care units, I would imagine that the world of the unseen would be running rampant.

Therefore, it was with little surprise that while doing research for this book, I found a brief story on the internet from the daughter of a respected nurse, working the graveyard shift at the Women's Pavilion at Sparrow Hospital.

The nurse was standing at the nurses' station filling out paperwork when she decided to check on a certain patient. Still having her head buried in a patient's chart, she proceeded to walk down the main hallway. In her peripheral vision, she could make out a female patient in a hospital gown making her way toward her. Finally looking up from her paperwork, she noted an unknown female patient in her fifties with her hair done up in a bun. Before the nurse could question this patient as to why she was out of bed, the patient walked right through her with numbing coldness, and then vanished. Convinced she was losing her mind, the nurse sat down in a nearby chair to regain her composure, and decided she would not mention her experience to her coworkers.

After several days, the nurse pushed herself to talk about her experience with the other nurses, only to find that none of them was surprised. She discovered that paranormal activity was common on this ward and was informed that several patients often complained about a little boy, who kept bouncing a ball around in the rooms. Although the staff keeps looking, no little boy has ever been found in any of the patients' rooms.

14
The Ghosts
That Got Away

While doing research for a book, we often came across public references to locations that were reported to be experiencing paranormal phenomena; however, we rarely found anything more than a mere mention. In many of these cases research into the case also yielded no information to support a haunting or even part of the rumored history. Most times, no one other than the articles' authors has knowledge of the reported events, and there were typically no witnesses to anything resembling strange or unexplained occurrences.

This chapter is all about the stories and "leads" that never panned out. Even without the benefit of a complete history, these locations are still believed by many to be haunted and therefore we believe they deserve mention in this book.

Paris Avenue

This short story came to us from a neighbor of those in a haunted home. The source told us about an event that occurred late one night while their neighbors were watching television. The neighbors were enjoying a quiet evening at home when they heard a loud thud against the door leading upstairs. The neighbor stated that he and his wife went to investigate and stood in terror as they watched the doorknob turning, but the door never opened. The friend stated that their neighbors were so disturbed by the event that they rarely ever talk about it. Apparently, that was true.

East Lansing Home

This information came in the form of a posting on a local message board. We were unable to talk personally with the submitter, and this may have something to do with the fact that the person actually lives in the home. This may have something to do with the fact that the person claims to live in the residence.

This submitter mentioned strange occurrences that were constantly taking place in the home such as light bulbs burning out at an alarming rate. Most of us know that burning out light bulbs is more of a sign of bad wiring and cheap light bulbs, but this person also mentioned that someone unseen would turn off the stove whenever they would turn it on. Whoever was cooking would turn on the stove and leave the area only to return and discover the dial had been turned to the OFF position.

More strange nuisances were the television set turning on and off and an occasional cold spot felt.

The Haunted Carriage

This was a small mention from the town of Dansville, Michigan. It was a simple and tiny statement about a spectral carriage that is seen moving down a certain road at night. The exact road could never be located, nor the origin of the carriage itself.

Bancroft Park

The sad apparition of a pregnant woman has been spotted near a sizeable boulder in this park off Indiana Avenue. No information could be found on who this unknown woman is or why she would haunt this area. In addition, I could not pinpoint the exact location of the sightings in this park.

Jones Lake

Just south of West Sheridan Road, Jones Lake appears to have its own ghostly tale. A quick email that was sent briefly talked about the ghostly apparition of a young male, sitting on the banks and fishing during the early morning hours. The unexplained entity is seen wearing a winter coat. This phantom can be watched for only a few seconds before he will disappear.

Research could not turn up a death at Jones Lake, especially in the wintertime.

Phantom Dancers

This is another local tale from outside the city of Dansville. If you follow down Clark Road, eventually, you will come to a dead end. Off to one side at the end of this road, you will see a field that is rumored to hold a specter's ball.

Legend tells of seeing the eerie shadows of "people" dancing in the distance. Generations have wondered if what they were viewing was not a residual haunting. Could these be the images of a coven of witches or a satanic cult from decades past, performing the same phantom ritual, over and over again?

Genessee Neighborhood

In 2001, the Genessee Neighborhood Association hosted a very different Halloween event—not commercialized haunted houses designed for quick scares, but a walking ghost tour. This distinctive event introduced certain houses, all filled with stories about supernatural activity.

The ghostly tour marched guests past houses built in the 1800s and through the oldest neighborhood in the Lansing. The tour began at Ferris Park on the corner of Pine and West Genessee Streets, and participants were lead past four old houses where true ghost stories were told for each home.

The first house on this tour was 897 Shiawassee Street, where the tour guide talked about Henry Prichette and his dog Max. Prichette fell into a deep depression after the death of his wife, and neighbors never saw the man or his dog outside of the house again. Both eventually died and many people are convinced their spirits became part of the house forever. People in the neighborhood have claimed to see the ghost Prichette walking around the driveway with his phantom dog to this day.

The only other house publicly mentioned was 713 West Genessee Street; however, there is no description of the ethereal story behind neither this house nor the other two houses on the tour was mentioned in this State News article. Other homes on the street were a part of the tour as well, though the specific stories were not available to us. But we think it's safe to say that the Genessee neighborhood has some haunting good ghosts on their tour. (Check with the Genessee Neighborhood Association for schedules.)

The Victorian Lady

The historic regions of downtown Lansing are riddled with century-old houses, now converted into businesses. Becky, along with her friends James and Kathy, met up with Kathy's mom and Robert, her mother's boyfriend, at Robert's insurance company. The three teenagers decided to take a break and sit on the inside stairway to wait when an unusual noise caught their attention. Turning to look behind them, they were startled to see an older lady in a Victorian dress, with her hair piled high on her head. The female entity stood looking at them for several seconds, turned, and walked up the staircase. Too stunned to do more than stare at the apparition, they watched as the old woman disappeared before their eyes, third step from the top.

Hope Middle School

Ten miles south of the most haunted college in Michigan (MSU) sits a middle school riddled with ghostly urban legends. Hope Middle School in Holt, Michigan, looks like any typical middle school, but current and past students claim that it is *nothing but* normal on the inside.

While doing research about the paranormal activity that is testified to occur here, I came across various versions of the ghost story surrounding this school.

The most popular version circulating throughout the internet is the 1980s tale of a young girl who was killed by a hall gate that slammed down, crushing her skull. The eerie sounds of the girl screaming is claimed to be heard every March 7th, the anniversary of her death.

Further digging into this story turned up references that the girl was not killed by an unpredictable gate, but by drowning in the deep end of the school's pool, located in the basement. This story has sparked many testimonies of sightings of the apparition in the basement.

A former janitor reported he saw her on several occasions, and she was witnessed by thirteen separate students in the girl's locker room, also in the basement. This janitor told members of the student body that the girl's name was Kara.

Other rumors consist of a lady who died of a heart attack; her spirit roams the stage to this day, and two students (a couple), had snuck in into the basement and were accidentally locked in a room under the pool. The doomed students died there of dehydration and their bodies were discovered several weeks later.

An Internet newspaper search did not produce any mention of deaths at this middle school. and emails to teachers at the school could not support the claims of student deaths.The next step was contacting the National School Safety and Security Administration. This organization records and documents all student deaths that have taken place at any elementary, secondary, or high school throughout the United States. The representative could not find any record of a student death occurring while this middle school has been in operation, or even while it was previously a high school.

Despite the facts that state otherwise, citizens of Holt still claim to see the ghostly apparition of this young girl, and are forced to listen to the sounds of her screams emanating throughout the middle school halls.

Old Schoolhouse

I found a quick reference to a former 100-year old schoolhouse on State Road in Lansing, which has been turned into a shop. Further research put me in touch with a woman who was part owner of a business located there in 1993.

This business owner, "Ann," declared that she had heard that, when the building was utilized as a school, a janitor employed by the school district had committed suicide in the building.

One episode sticks in Ann's memory. While working late, preparing for the grand opening of her business, she had her six-year-old daughter accompany her to the building. Upon leaving, the six year old questioned her mom about the other cars in the driveway. Ann explained that the other vehicles belonged to the florist next door. The little girl quickly responded that she thought one of the cars must belong to the janitor.

Surprised, Ann corrected her daughter by stating that the building does not have a janitor. Not to be misunderstood by her mother, the girl replied, "Yes there is. I saw him tonight."

Ann knew that she never discussed the historical rumor about the janitor's suicide with or in front of her daughter. With curiosity, she questioned her daughter further."Where did you see him?"

The young child stated that the man was standing at the stairs. When asked by the mother if the man said anything to her, the daughter replied, "No, he just waved at me and smiled."

Ann was never sure if the man her daughter saw was the spirit of the former janitor, but it always remained in the back of her mind while she was in the building.

15
Capitol UFOs

The Capital of Michigan seems to be as popular for UFOs as it is with ghosts. Citizens and visitors have reported everything from streaks dancing across the sky to triangle-shaped crafts that hover above buildings and homes. The following are excerpts from real eyewitness accounts from the National UFO Reporting Center of reported sightings in and around the Lansing area. To protect privacy, all names have been withheld by the Reporting Center.

Summer 1952

This is the oldest report that is listed on the National UFO Reporting Center's website for the Lansing area.

"I was 9 years old at the time. My parents were visiting my aunt and uncle and playing cards inside the house. They lived in a little four corners community about 20 miles northwest of Lansing, Michigan. It's too small to be listed on maps or have its own zip code. I was out in the back yard laying on my back looking at the stars, trying to make them into pictures. As for the exact time, it was dark so was some time after 9:00 pm and before 11:00 pm, which was when we left to drive home. As I was watching the stars, one of them moved. It quickly went from one place in the sky to another and then

stopped. The route it traveled was like a large U. There were no flames, no noise, no brightening or dimming of its light, no blinking. It just moved. It was definitely not a plane, helicopter or other type of aircraft. Even at 9 years old, I was very familiar with and had ridden in most types of aircraft, I spent many Saturday afternoons at the airport just watching and bugging the private pilots for a ride. I've seen shooting stars and it was definitely not one of those. It was definitely not a meteor; they do not make U turns."

July 1970

"It was mid-Summer in my home town, Lansing, Michigan, and my best friend and I were playing softball with some other kids at the neighborhood school ground. When it started getting too dark for softball, we walked back to our street. When we got to my house, the stars had just begun to come out. I went in the house and grabbed a couple sodas and went back outside. We both laid back on the grass of the front lawn next to the driveway, looking up into the sky. At the same time, we both saw a stationary point of light that was a blue-green color. It wasn't overly bright, but it was larger than any star I had ever seen."

"We watched it for maybe fifteen minutes. During that time, it wasn't doing much, other than pulsating slightly, but then, we started seeing faint orange glittery streaks of light shooting from it."

June 1979

"As myself, my brother and 2 friends were walking home; I glanced into the ski and saw what looked like a crumpled piece of plastic floating in the sky like a wind-blown tarp. As I watched it I realized it was not moving and had kind of a haze around it. This was on a clear sunny day and I don't think there was a cloud in the sky. It was a gray silver in color and had no lights. As I watched, it took off from a stand still, to out of sight in just a second or two. It shot up at slight angle went straight for an airliner flying over head and then out of sight."

November 1980

"I was in the southern to middle part of town waiting outside of a friend's house for my wife as we were leaving and just looking at the sky when I noticed a dark object lit by the city lights float by for about 15 seconds before it disappeared in the dark. It was rectangular and had

distinct sections best described as the sections of a large tootsie roll. It had no wings or lights. It silently and smoothly went by almost overhead west of where I was. I would estimate the size by the amount of light to the duration to be larger than a train box car."

December 1995

"Man and wife were standing under the overhang of their house. Husband looks up and sees 5 'pinkish' objects in a clear area of the western sky, that appeared to be very high and traveling very fast. Objects were in a staggered-V formation, with one object on one side, four objects forming the other arm of the V. Objects traversed approximately 45 degrees of sky in 5 sec. They were very precisely spaced from one another."

Note by author - The observer is former FAA ATC, and is pilot.

August 1997

"I was outside letting my cat in the house when I saw these lights outside my house in the middle of the night. This weird looking craft, which was extremely bright, was hovering. I saw it at about 500 ft.! I could feel intense heat coming off of whatever it was. Then it just bolted out of there, and appeared in a different part of the sky."

March 1999

"I was driving my vehicle up a ramp westbound when something caught my eye to the south-south-east. It was too large to be a meteorite and though it moved slower than one, it moved much faster than an airplane. It then dropped below sight. It was a white ball of light."

November 1999

"I noticed a green flare-like object streaking from the SWW to the NEE at 7 pm. At first I thought it was a firework, but it was maintaining a horizontal path from horizon to horizon. I would characterize it as something entering the atmosphere except it appeared to be lower than normal 747 style traffic, or it was quite large, but the detail in the flame would make me believe that it was closer to the ground that far away. Also there where small orange lights coming out the back. I believed it to be ember-type material breaking away, but the lights fell directly back, one at a time, evenly spaced and they didn't fall away as I would expect waste material to do. They were evenly spaced and fell directly behind the object, but still seemed to be keeping up with the green flame, which is why I think it was not just a meteorite. I was in my car pulling out of a coffee shop at the time, so I don't know if it made noise. There were probably 10 to 15 people seated outside the coffee shop and I noticed that all of them were up and looking as well."

October 2000

"Several witnesses observed a bright white light moving very fast across the South Lansing sky. Bright, round, white light. Steady (non-flashing). Appeared to be low altitude. Moving from East to West far faster than a plane in a straight line. No sound. Clear cold night with a sliver of moon."

November 2000

"What I saw in the sky was 5-6 black diamond-shaped floating objects. They were flying in a synchronized fashion with a centralized somewhat larger black diamond shaped one in the middle. They were floating south-west to north-east right at the top of the tree tops. They were close enough to hear if they made a sound, but they were silent. It was a clear blue sky and it just so happened that when it flew by at about 35-40 miles an hour, no one else was on the road where I witnessed them. The smaller ones were about the size of about 3 full-size vans. The larger one was about 2-3 times bigger then the smaller ones."

April 2001

"I was walking around my town at night around 10:30 on April 13. I glanced up in the clear sky and saw a triangle formation of 3 saucer-shaped objects. The saucers flew overhead silently and very quickly. I have seen these saucers more times than I can remember in East Lansing. They seem to be a pretty common occurrence. They always fly silently, but at varying speeds. Sometimes they fly so fast it seems impossible."

May 2001

"I was out driving around at night and decided to pull over at the weigh station located just west of Lansing on I-96 heading westbound. The sky was clear and the stars were full and bright. I was looking toward the north at what seemed like just a collection of stars. Suddenly one of these "stars," broke formation and shot straight up. It started slow at first, then gained speed until it was out of sight. The object was bright white in color and did not pulse or change color."

September 15, 2001

"My father and I saw what looked like a star in the north western sky above Lansing at high noon. It sat in one spot for an hour then just disappeared. It looked metallic and could be seen even through the clouds as it passed. It was higher than the clouds since two jet planes flew below it. It never moved but all a sudden it was gone at around 1:30 pm."

September 21, 2001

"It was very high in the sky, too far for me to measure. It was reflecting in the sun but it wasn't moving. I looked about a few minutes later but it still hadn't moved."

Note from author: The September 15th and September 21st reports are strikingly similar. Both were sighted over Lansing by two separate people.

June 2002

"Outside on a clear sky watching the stars, I saw a satellite, and watched it move slowly away. No big deal. I saw another one, or so I thought, however this one moved sort of in a curve and faded out. I assumed its reflection of the sun had been blocked by the earth until I saw another one in the same eastern part of the sky. Then, when walking back to my main apartment door, I saw another one in the north, much brighter. It became very bright, like when a plane turns towards you. However this one, also disappeared."

November 2002

"On November 13, 2002, I saw what I think was a triangle UFO. First, when I went to bring my dog in, I saw it behind a tree. I saw what looked like a bright white light. Then when it started to move, I saw red and white lights. It was big and shaped like a triangle, but it made a sound like a plane or helicopter. Earlier I saw a plane and a small object and it look like the small object was chasing it."

July 2003

"I was west of downtown Lansing about 1.5 miles or so. I saw something traveling southbound over the trees and I would estimate that it was just east of downtown Lansing. It looked like a rectangle but could have been any shape as I was viewing it from the side. Lansing has an airport here and I see small and large commercial planes, but this had no features like they do, just rectangular with a sort of structure to it, like a triangular framework like steel beams or something.

It looked like it was on a downward angle but going away from the airport and it traveled very flat and quickly for its size. The 747s that I see seem to float along and this was moving probably 4 or 5 times faster than that. It appeared closer to the ground than commercial aircraft, too. I was driving my car and couldn't get much more than that. It disappeared behind the tree line and the GM Plant."

October 2004

"There was this formation with about 9 lights. It went very fast, and was pretty close to the earth. My friend and I were walking in the Nature Center of Lansing, and there is this clearing of trees; I looked up and saw it first, grabbed my friend, and he saw the tail end of it. It was a short experience but very strange."

March 2006

"I woke up to my dog whining to go outside at about 6:12 A.M. I let him out of my front door and I looked up and did a double take. I saw a disk-like shaped object flying in the sky. It had many lights on the underside, about ten of them. Two of them were red and the other lights were white. The object was very metallic looking. I know it wasn't an airplane because it was too low to the ground and too large. Also none of the lights were blinking. I saw it flying to the south. I froze and stared at it as it disappeared into the clouds."

July 2007

"We saw bright orange (like flame, not lights) teardrop-shaped objects moving roughly east in a straight line. On this evening, we saw two of them approximately five minutes apart. The evening was still, but we could hear no noise coming from them.

Five days prior, several of us saw three of these objects over about an hour's time."

Summary

After reading these few accounts, I could only begin to speculate how many sightings have gone unreported by witnesses for fear of ridicule.

The study of UFOs has rapidly grown and thanks in part to the media, it is now commonly accepted by society. If you are interested in the study and research of UFOs, please visit the following websites:

National UFO Reporting Center. http://www.ufocenter.com
Mutual UFO Network. http://www.mufon.com/

16
Theories
Behind A Haunting

After reading all the stories in this book, many of you are likely wondering what causes a place to be haunted. There are many theories; I am going to discuss a few of the most commonly accepted ones.

Let us start with the most common and most widely accepted reasons a place would be haunted. I would be willing to bet that every one of you reading this have at one point in your life been to a location where someone, who died suddenly, is rumored to be haunting the site of the death. While the cause of this haunting might seem obvious, it is important to consider the difference in the two main types of hauntings: intelligent and residual.

An intelligent haunting is defined as any haunting in which the ghost or spirit is able to interact with the living. In contrast, a residual haunting is when an event is replayed the same way each time the ghosts are present.

In the intelligent haunting following a sudden death, there may be many reasons the spirit has remained on Earth. I am going to touch on a few.

The ghost could be trapped in this world and unable to cross over because they are not aware they are dead.

The Spirit might have a major piece of unfinished business.
They might be unwilling to leave a loved one.
They might want to fix an injustice done to them in life.

Residual hauntings are not even considered by most paranormal investigators to be ghosts in the truest sense, but rather a psychic imprint similar to a video tape. Video tapes capture images on film—an oxidized film. Many building materials, such as slate, marble, and iron have similar properties to this film. When the traumatic event occurs, these materials record the event for future playback. When an unknown trigger starts the playback, we see the event happen, as if the participants were in the room with us.

Another type of haunting is known as a portal haunting. Portals are thought to be doorways to another world or dimension in which entities travel through. These portals can be found in many places, and normally involve several different hauntings in a single location. In a portal haunting, you might witness odd creatures, bright balls of lights, or floating objects in addition to the normal human ghosts. No one knows what causes portal hauntings, but it is a commonly accepted theory that the use of Ouija board can, and most investigators at one time or another have witnessed this cause and effect.

It is also possible and much more common than most people might think to conjure the dead. The word conjure normally brings images of Merlin working a magic spell, and in reality this is very much what is done to create these hauntings. Conjured haunting are most commonly attributed to people, untrained in the magical arts, attempting to follow a spell they read in a book, or on a Web site. Most of the people that conjure these spirits do not even truly believe it is possible and are just messing around.

That leaves us with one other major type of haunting, the one that I find the most fascinating, the poltergeist haunting. Most researches no longer think of poltergeist hauntings as ghosts, but there is still much disagreement about what they really are.

One theory is that hauntings, especially poltergeists hauntings, are from the human subconscious. In early 1970s a group of paranormal researchers known as the Toronto Society for Psychical Research conducted an experiment to try to prove this theory. They wanted to know if they could create a ghost. The idea was to invent an imaginary character, and then conduct séances to contact him or better yet get him to appear to them.

They gathered a group of average people with no claims of psychic ability from all occupations. The group included the former Chairperson of MENSA, a homemaker, an accountant, a bookkeeper, and a college student.

They wrote a brief biography of his life a segment of which I have included here:

Philip was an aristocratic Englishman, living in the middle 1600s at the time of Oliver Cromwell. He had been a supporter of the King, and was a Catholic. He was married to a beautiful but cold and frigid wife, Dorothea, the daughter of a neighboring nobleman.

One day when out riding on the boundaries of his estates Philip came across a gypsy encampment and saw there a beautiful dark-eyed raven-haired gypsy girl, Margo, and fell instantly in love with her. He brought her back secretly to live in the gatehouse, near the stables of Diddington Manor—his family home.

For some time he kept his love-nest secret, but eventually Dorothea, realizing he was keeping someone else there, found Margo, and accused her of witchcraft and stealing her husband. Philip was too scared of losing his reputation and his possessions to protest at the trial of Margo, and she was convicted of witchcraft and burned at the stake.

Philip was subsequently stricken with remorse that he had not tried to defend Margo and used to pace the battlements of Diddington in despair. Finally, one morning his body was found at the bottom of the battlements, whence he had cast himself in a fit of agony and remorse.

The plan was to have several meetings in which they would discuss the life of Philip, concentrate on him, and see if he would start to appear to them. After about a year with limited success, they decided to use another approach.

They conducted the cliché séance, the room was darkened, and objects that would be near and dear to Philip were brought in and placed on the table that they all sat around; they joined hands. Soon they began to get a response, in the form of taps on the table. After several sessions he was able to answer questions in this way: One tap meant yes, two meant no.

After a while, he was able to do more than just tap, he was able to move objects, some as large as the table, which he would at times make balance on one leg.

They devised a test to see if they had contacted Philip or if they had indeed contacted a departed spirit. In this test, they would ask several questions of the entity: They wanted to know if he had knowledge outside that of their own about his time. He did not. Philip could never answer a single question that the group did not know the answer to proving the answers were from their own subconscious.

Philips abilities did not stop with knocking; he was able to turn lights on and off, and once, in front of an audience of over fifty people and a television crew, he even levitated a table.

I, for one, have investigated many poltergeist cases and have found that the majority of them start after someone in the house becomes convinced there is a haunting. Is this the basis for a poltergeist haunting? Many researchers say yes; others have a different idea.

To them poltergeist can be best explained as psychokinetic ability being involuntarily harnessed by the victim of the haunting. In these cases, the victim is usually an adolescent girl, and the attacks often very violent.

This theory became popular in the 1930s when parapsychologist Nador Fodor was able to show a correlation between repressed anger, hostility, sexual tension, and poltergeist disturbances.

In the 1960s, the Psychical Research Foundation of Durham furthered this research and found the following. In the cases that they labeled "recurrent spontaneous psychokinesis" (RSPK), which they defined as inexplicable, spontaneous physical effects, generally, they discovered, the most common agent was a child or teenager whose unwitting PK was a way of expressing hostility without the fear of punishment. The individual was not aware of being the cause of such disturbances, but was, at the same time, secretly or openly pleased that they occurred. Modern research has even shown that, in many cases, poltergeist activity can be stopped by psychological treatment.

Though no one is truly an expert in the paranormal field until they themselves pass away, more theories will come to light as time goes on. Regardless of the reason why a haunting occurs, people never forget when it happens to them.

Appendix

Haunted Geocaching

Geocaching is a high-tech treasure hunting game played throughout the world by adventure seekers equipped with GPS devices. The basic idea is to locate hidden containers, called geocaches, outdoors and then share your experiences online. Geocaching is enjoyed by people from all age groups, with a strong sense of community and support for the environment. You can find more information at http://www.geocaching.com.

There are many geocaches placed throughout the state of Michigan, and sometimes are hidden at haunted locations.

Below is a list of geocaches that are hidden, by *Paranormal Lansing* authors and other geocaching members that coincide with some of the locations in this book.

Find one of the geocaches below and maybe you will have a paranormal experience while you are there!

Geocaches placed by *Paranormal Lansing* authors:

Blood Cemetery,GC1EE1T
http://www.geocaching.com/seek/cache_details.aspx?guid=8992e31b-5b1d-4155-ba7e-e1e58442a1e1

Witch Of Seven Gables,GC1CE4T
http://www.geocaching.com/seek/cache_details.aspx?guid=87838078-5f08-4e62-8217-a3c69f77d1e8

Other caches hidden at haunted locations listed in this book:

Red Cedar River (MSU Campus),GC15XKD
http://www.geocaching.com/seek/cache_details.aspx?wp=GC15XKD

MSU Multi (Throughout the north portion of campus),GC62C7
http://www.geocaching.com/seek/cache_details.aspx?pf=&guid=199d259b-3ebf-4b3d-9b25-a5b53b33a913&decrypt=y&log=&numlogs

Horticulture Garden (MSU),GC1D524
http://www.geocaching.com/seek/cache_details.aspx?wp=GC1D524

911 Memorial (former Hotel Kern site),GC6QWJ
http://www.geocaching.com/seek/cache_details.aspx?wp=GCGQWJ

Bibliography

Bartner, Amy. "Sentences Handed Out In Blair Case." *The State News*, June 20, 2002.

Beyond Investigations. "Bath School Disaster Memorial Park Investigation." http://www.thebeyond.info/hunts/bathbomg.htm. July 29, 2006. Accessed on July 2007.

City Of The Silent. "Timeline For Taphophiles." http://gazissax.best.vwh.net/silence/cemtime/time5.html. Accessed on July 2008.

Clinton County Historical Society. *Clinton County History*. 1980 edition

Davis, Amy. "Fact Or Fiction." *The State News,* August 15, 2003.

Dear, William. *The Dungeon Master: The Disappearance of James Dallas Egbert III.* Ballantine Books, October 12, 1985.

DeVries, Corinne; Foley, Aaron; McCormick, Ryan; Mehta, Benita; Phillips, Lauren; and Wayne Guite, Jacqueline. "*31 Ways To Celebrate Halloween.*" *The State News*, October 27, 2005.

Doe, Becka. "The Victorian Lady." Ghost Mysteries Website submission. August 1, 2008.

Doe, Christy. "Regretfully." http://www.ghosm.com/truestories4.htm. Ghost Hunters Of Southern Michigan. Accessed in November 2007.

Ellsworth, MJ. *The Bath School Disaster.* (Publisher Unknown) 1927.

Foley, Aaron. "Cadavers Replaced Students In Dorm." *The State News*, April 13, 2004.

Forsyth, Kevin. "History of East Lansing and MSU." http://kevinforsyth.net/ELMI/.Accessed in April 2008.

Frye, Megan. "Tracking The Tunnels." *The State News*, April 23, 2003.

Galek, Florence. "The Story Of Mary Kate." GlobalPsychics.com. Accessed on July 2008.

Godfrey, Linda. *Weird Michigan.* Sterling Publishing, July 25, 2006.

Gopwani, Jewel. "Examiner Identifies Body Found in MSU Residence Hall." *The Michigan Daily.* September 27, 1999.

Grand Rapids Press. "Dynamite Explosion Kills 39 In Bath School, Near Lansing." Grand Rapids, Michigan. May 18, 1927.

Grand Rapids Press. "Kehoe's Vengeance Toll Now 43." Grand Rapids, Michigan. May 19, 1927.

Guenther, Heather. "Ghost Hunters To Take Students On Campus Tour." *The State News*, October 22, 2007.

Gumbrecht, Jamie. "Divers Continue to Comb River for Reported Body." *The State News,* October 23, 2001.

Harmon, Katelyn. "Olivet College Historical Facts: Tragedies, Triumphs, and Firsts." *Olivet College Echo*, October 19, 2007.

Hately, Shaun. "The Disappearance Of James Dallas Egbert III." *Places To Go, People To Be*, 1999.

Homes, Vance. http://www.vanceholmes.com/court/trial_missing_students.html. Accessed in August 2007.

Hunter, Gerald S. "Haunted Michigan: Recent Encounters with Active Spirits." *Lake Claremont Press*, October 18, 2000.

Hunter, Gerald S. "More Haunted Michigan: New Encounters With Ghosts of the Great Lakes State." *Thunder Bay Press*, February 14, 2005.

Jordan, Don. "In Search of the Paranormal." *The State News*, October 30, 2003.

Keeping, Juliana. "Things That Go Bump In The Night." *The State News*, October 25, 2001.

Lanier, Yvette. "Who Ya Gonna Call? Ghost Hunters." *The State News*, October 25, 2006.

LeBeau, Emilie. "Find The Paranormal With These Tips." *The Lowdown: Lansing's Entertainment Guide.* October 25, 2006.

Leebove, Laura. "Lansing Museum Showcases City's Unique Automotive Past." *The State News*. January 15, 2008.

Looby, Katie. "Rooming With A Dead Teacher." *The Big Green* — vol. 4, November 1, 2005.

McGinnis, Carol. *Michigan Genealogy Sources & Resource.* Genealogical Publishing Company, 2nd Edition. April 30, 2005.

Michigan State University. http://www.msu.edu. Accessed in 2007.

Monk, Rich. "Odd Coincidences Abound On Campus." *The State News*, October 26, 2001.

MSU Message boards. http://www.spartantailgate.com. Accessed April 2007 — March 2008.

New York Times, The. "Maniac Blows Up School, Kills 42, Mostly Children; Had Protested High Taxes." May 19, 1927.

Oaks Yearbook, The. *Q&A: With Alpha Lambda Epsilon.* Olivet Colege: Greek Life. 2004-05.

Olivet College. http://www.olivetcollege.edu. Accessed in May 2008.

Oprean, Amy. "Have You Seen Mary?" *The State News*, October 31, 2006.

ParaHaunt. "Bath Investigation." http://www.miparahaunt.com. June 15, 2002. Accessed on July 2007.

Political Graveyard, The. http://politicalgraveyard.com/bio/mayne-mcallen.html. Perry Mayo Obituary.

Poor House Story. *History of Shiawassee and Clinton Counties.* D.W. Ensign & Co., 1880.

RE Olds Transportation Museum website. http://www.reoldsmuseum.org. Accessed May and July 2008.

Rothwell, W.P. "Why I Am Interested in Ghosts!" http://www.geocities.com/CapeCanaveral/Lab/7746/strange.html?20075. Accessed in May 2008.

Schimpf, Sheila. "Haunted Homes." *Lansing State Journal*, October 31, 1997.

Sparty Secrets. "How Did Mayo Hall Become Haunted?" October 2007.

State Journal, The. "Raze Walls To Start Hunting Dead." Lansing, Michigan. December 11, 1934.

Stewart, Joseph. "The Paranormal Nomad: Case #522." http://www.theparanormalnomad.org/grc/522/0001_c522.html. January 19, 2007.

Stewart, Joseph. "The Paranormal Nomad: Case #700." http://www.theparanormalnomad.org/grc/522/0001_c700.html. October 22, 2007.

Strange USA. http://www.strangeusa.com. Accessed in June 2007-June 2008.

The Shadowlands. "Michigan's Haunted Places." http://www.theshadowlands.com. Accessed in 2007

Turner, Kris. "Human Remains Found, Identity Unknown." *The State News*, June 16, 2005.

Underground Railroad In Michigan. http://www.motopera.org/mg_ed/educational/UndergroundRR.html. Accessed in April 2008.

Walters, Patrick. "Ghosts, Folklore Haunted 'U.'" *The State News*, October 31, 2002.

Weird Dansville website. Accessed on December 2007.

Wikipedia. "Lansing, MI." http://en.wikipedia.org/wiki/Lansing_%28MI%29#History. Accessed on April 2007.

Wikipedia. "Ransom E. Olds." http://en.wikipedia.org/wiki/Ransom_Olds. Accessed on September 2007.

Wyant, Rebecca. "The Burning Bed." Term Paper Access.

Zoglin, Richard. "Domestic Reign Of Terror." *Time Magazine*, October 8, 1984.

Zuko, Von. *North American Hauntings and Unexplained Phenomena: Olivet College.* 1998

Index